ḤÁJÍ MÍRZÁ ḤAYDAR-'ALÍ WITH SHOGHI EFFENDI
as a boy. Standing behind them are Mírzá
Maḥmúd-i-Zarqání and Khusraw, the gardener.

Stories from

The Delight of Hearts

Stories from

THE DELIGHT OF HEARTS

The Memoirs of Ḥájí Mírzá Ḥaydar-'Alí

translated from the original Persian
and abridged
by

A. Q. FAIZI

KALIMÁT PRESS
LOS ANGELES

First Edition

Library of Congress Cataloging in Publication Data

Ḥaydar-'Alí.
Stories from The delight of hearts.

1. Ḥaydar-'Alí. 2. Bahaism—Biography. I. Faizi, Abu'l-Qásim. II. Title.
BP395.H39A2513 1980 297'.8961 79-91219
ISBN 0-933770-11-1

Manufactured in the United States of America

FOREWORD

One of the most thrilling aspects of Bahá'í history is the story of the many waiting souls who embraced the Faith manifested by the Báb and Bahá'u'lláh. These souls appear in every clime and in every stratum of life. For them it is sufficient merely to behold a ray of the Sun and they exclaim, "We believe." With the slightest movement of a finger, the veils are drawn aside and such souls become illumined by the light of the Divine Message.

Ḥájí Mírzá Ḥaydar-'Alí was one such person. He was born in Iṣfahán, where his father was one of the well-known dignitaries of the Muslim community and a prominent member of the Shaykhí sect. As such, he endeavored to give his son the most suitable education of that time. The Ḥájí pursued the normal Islamic curriculum, which included the Qur'án, the Arabic language, interpretation, jurisprudence, and rhetoric.

As a young man, the Ḥájí stood firm as he faced the baffling problems of life. It seemed that a certain mysterious power gave him the strength to remain steadfast and staunch against all sufferings and afflictions, including repeated exiles and imprisonment in horrible dungeons. When he reached the prime of his youth, there was no question about his moral strength and spiritual uprightness.

Someone mentioned to him the news of the advent of the Qá'im, and Ḥájí Mírzá Ḥaydar-'Alí plunged himself in the Ocean of the new Revelation. Thereafter, he faced nothing but tribulation, adversity, exile, and imprisonment. Never did he retaliate, nor did he manifest any sign of hostility or desire for retribution. Time and again, he faced the storms which raged about him and drew him into the vortex of misery. And yet, invariably, he was always ready to receive all blows with thanksgiving and radiant acquiescence.

Finally the beloved Master, 'Abdu'l-Bahá, invited him to the Holy Land, where he lived to the end of his life. Letters often came to Haifa requesting the Ḥájí's presence in the eastern countries where the believers regarded with great affection this veteran soldier of the Army of Life. But 'Abdu'l-Bahá refused, often covering the Ḥájí with His own cloak and embracing him, repeating, "Ḥájí is ours. Ḥájí is ours."

During the long years of the Ḥájí's imprisonment, the attendants used to shave the heads of all the prisoners. And of course he was included. It became a habit of his to shave his head each day, and he continued to do so even after his release. One day, in Haifa, the Ḥájí complained of eye trouble. The beloved Master spontaneously advised him, "Do not shave your head anymore. Try each day to write a few pages."

Our Ḥájí followed these instructions strictly, and the sweet fruit of this daily exercise is the book which you are about to read.

A. Q. Faizí

Stories from The Delight of Hearts

THE FRIENDS HAVE often asked me how I first came in contact with the Faith and finally embraced it. The explanation is this: during my life, in Iran, I often saw people mercilessly persecuted, often tortured and beaten to death. Sometimes I saw people hanged by their ears or their hands and pelted with stones. Curious as to why such terrible punishments were being inflicted on these individuals, I approached many people and asked them about it. But the only answer I received was this: "They are Bábís."

My own spiritual quest had led me to many cities in Iran. I would enter a city and seek out all the religious leaders there. But I was always disappointed. While staying in Iṣfahán, I was invited one night to a garden. The men who were present talked about various subjects. Somehow the subject of the Báb and His religion was raised, and I took the opportunity to speak. "This person made two great mistakes," I said. "Therefore, he was unable to accomplish his goals and was destroyed. First, he set himself against the established authorities, and, second, he tried to overturn the customs and beliefs of the masses. He should have allied himself with one or the other of these factions in order to gather support for his cause."

One of those present responded politely, "If this was a mistake, then it has been made by all the Prophets of God, including Muḥammad, the Seal of the Prophets, and all the Holy Imáms."

I was surprised by this answer and also embarrassed

that I had made such a false and simpleminded statement. I also realized that the one who answered me must be a Bábí and that there must be more to the Bábí Cause than I had previously thought.

I decided to become friends with this person, which was no easy task since all Bábís were in grave danger and had to be extremely cautious. Nonetheless, he eventually adopted me as his student, though he was at first afraid that I might be insincere in my quest. Fearful of the consequences of revealing his own inner convictions, he scarcely told me anything. Although he did not speak of the Cause, he was preparing the ground for a sacred and fruitful conversation, and gradually I won his confidence.

It happened one day that I saw a large crowd gathered in one of the squares of the city. I was attracted by the noise and commotion and drew closer. There I saw five siyyids, mullás, and merchants, well dressed and from the respectable classes. Their ears had been nailed to a post, and soldiers were beating them with sticks, demanding that they recant their faith. I was amazed that, even in that desperate condition, those believers were calm and patient and thankful. They refused to recant and quoted passages from the Qur'án to prove the claims of their Prophet, the Báb.

As I observed their steadfastness and submission to the Will of God, the fire of search was inflamed within me and I caught a glimpse of the grandeur of this Cause.

After I had become intimate with my friend, and when he was assured of my sincerity, he revealed to me that he was a Bábí, and we began to discuss the Faith. We were afraid of being discovered, so we could not meet openly. The times and places of our meetings kept shifting. Some nights he would invite me to his house—but always after midnight. When I entered the house, I had to hide myself in the corridor until we were sure that all the members of the household were in bed and sound asleep. Then, and only then, would my friend come for me and conduct me quietly to the kitchen. There we would study the Báb's Writings and chant prayers. At times, when it was too dark and we were unable to see the words, the only thing we could do was place a candle on the floor of the oven, then hold up the Writings to the light and, with great difficulty, study them.

When my friend came to my house, it was with the same secrecy. Sometimes it would become even more difficult. We could not have meetings of more than three or four persons, and then only late at night. Once, I rented the upper room of a certain house. My room had a window that opened on the garden. So that the people in the house would not know where I went at night, I used to climb down from the window by a rope tied to the iron bars, and return to my room the same way before sunrise to sleep.

MY FATHER was not a believer. He was a Shaykhí and a follower of Ḥájí Muḥammad Karím Khán.[1] He was firmly against my Faith and would follow me to many places to voice his opposition to my beliefs. We exchanged some letters, but they did not help. Eventually he left Kirmán in quest of me and found me in the small town of Ná'ín. He hoped that there he would be able to educate and guide me, since most of the people of the town were followers of Karím Khán.

My father went to the governor of the town, whom he knew personally, and asked for me to be brought to him. I was summoned to the governor's house. But with the assistance of God, I was able to speak in a manner that pleased everyone. They all encouraged me and spoke words of approval. "The grace of Ḥájí Muḥammad Karím Khán has encircled you and protected you," they said. "He has not allowed you to go astray."

Every morning it was their custom to recite verses from the Qur'án after prayers. It was my honor to recite these verses, and everyone was always pleased to hear those beautiful words. To open the way for our discussion, I began to include verses of the Báb with those from the Qur'án. No one criticized—or even detected that verses other than those from the Qur'án were being chanted. This gave me an opportunity to present my argument to the people in the room, particularly my father.

An uncle of mine, Ḥájí Muḥammad-'Alí, lived in Ná'ín. He was a good friend of mine and knew of my correspondence with my father. So I asked him if he would be willing to hide me and protect me and take me secretly to Iṣfahán. He accepted, and I prepared to leave.

I went to the hall where my father and the governor and several other people were seated. I sat next to my father and said to him, "Suppose I had been born blind and could not know you by sight. Could I not certainly recognize you by your voice?"

"What is your aim in asking this question?" he responded.

"Let me finish the premise; then you will comprehend the purpose of my question," I replied. "Suppose, again, that you were to go on an extensive trip and return home only after a long time. I shall still know you by your voice and shall naturally run to you. When I receive kindness, compassion, and love, I shall know for certain that the newcomer is my father."

All present agreed, "This is true. It is obvious and understandable."

"Now, here is my question," I continued. "When I

chanted the verses of the Qur'án for you, I often included in the texts verses revealed by the Báb. I am sure you recognize the verses of the Prophet Muḥammad by His words, tone, and style. Then, why did no one protest? Surely, only because the words revealed by the Báb have the same tone, vigor, and style, and come from the same Source."

This concluded the discussion. I left the hall quickly and made for my uncle's house. I stayed in his house for a month, until all efforts to find me were exhausted. Then I secretly left Ná'ín and traveled to Iṣfahán.

My father and others came to Iṣfahán looking for me, and there they made efforts to have me killed or imprisoned. But the Ḥujjatu'l-Islám,[2] Siyyid Asadu'lláh, was a very influential man in Iṣfahán and was related to me through my mother. The followers of Karím Khán were rejected by the prominent 'ulamá in Iṣfahán, and the two groups were openly hostile to one another. Seeing only that I was opposed to these people whom they hated, the 'ulamá protected me. My enemies were defeated, and I was victorious. But when my father died, I learned that he had disinherited me.

In Iṣfahán, I spent most of my time in the presence of Zaynu'l-Muqarrabín.[3] We used to go to distant and desolate places far from the tumult of the towns and villages, just to be together, study the Writings, chant prayers, and discuss the Cause of God. These moments of joy kept us alive, but we longed to teach and make His Name known in any way we could.

We tried different methods of approach. We went to an Indian who claimed to have some medical knowledge, and Jináb-i-Zayn [4] opened the discussion by saying, "I feel a painful sensation in my heart. I know of no physician who can help me."

"What is the cause?" asked the physician.

Jináb-i-Zayn replied, "A few days ago, I was walking in the street when suddenly I beheld a strange sight. Some people, held captive and helpless in the hands of a savage mob, were being tortured and mercilessly persecuted. I was so disturbed and alarmed that, ever since then, I have felt this pain in my heart." Then Jináb-i-Zayn went on to tell the Indian doctor about the Revelation of the Báb, His tragic history, and His Writings.

One day we were outside the city of Iṣfahán in a very pleasant place where there was a mosque and a stream and a few trees. We had taken provisions to spend the night. We went to the mosque, where we planned to stay. A few of the inhabitants were curious, so they entered the mosque and someone asked me where I was from. I had a slight Iṣfahání accent, but I said that I was from Shíráz.

"Why are you lying?" the man replied. "It is obvious that you are from Iṣfahán. Seventy thousand angels will curse a liar."

"Have you seen those angels?" I asked, hoping to create an opportunity to teach the Faith.

"Why shouldn't I have seen them?" he replied. "They are recorded in the authentic traditions of our Faith."

I was rather incautious and said, "Yes, I can tell that you have the spiritual discernment to have seen them."

Then they guessed our secret and immediately cried out, "These people are Bábís! Come and get them!" And we were forced to leave all of our belongings behind and run away.

These problems often occurred. There is one funny story about a certain siyyid who was a student in a religious school. I used to speak to him and I invited him to my home a few times. He claimed to have accepted the Faith. He got to know a few of the believers, and some of the Writings of the Báb were given to him.

Then someone informed me that the siyyid had said to him, "I have gotten to know some Bábís. When I meet all of them and find out what their schemes are, I plan to inform the authorities and have them all arrested."

The siyyid was living at the religious school at the time. So I went to the headmaster of the school and told him that he had a student who was a Bábí and was in possession of some of the Writings of the Báb. I also made sure that someone told the siyyid what I had done. When he heard this he was overtaken by fear, and, leaving all his belongings behind, he fled from the town and never returned.

A few years later, I was going from Shíráz to Búshihr. On the way, I stopped at a mosque in a small town, not knowing that this same siyyid now lived there. He saw me and recognized me. Seeing an opportunity to take his revenge, he approached me and said, "Do you remember what you did to me in Iṣfahán?"

"Yes," I replied. "You are that same Bábí student who was going to be arrested and killed in Iṣfahán. Now you have come here and have become a leader of Muslims in this mosque."

He was so frightened by my reply that the whole time I was in that place he would not leave my side, fearing that I would denounce him to others. He brought me food and tea until I left.

ALTHOUGH I WAS often persecuted in Iṣfahán and sometimes suffered great hardships, I was happy. I was in love with the Writings of the Báb, especially the Persian Bayán. Every day I would transcribe a portion of this book. In those days many were convinced that the advent of "Him Whom God shall make manifest" could not be far off. I used to say that if the Báb had not manifested Himself, then the Writings of Shaykh Aḥmad and Siyyid Káẓim [5] would have been left useless and unfulfilled. Now, similarly, if the Dispensation of the Báb were not followed by the Revelation of "Him Whom God shall make manifest," then the Writings of the Báb would have no purpose.

I did not like Azal.[6] I used to say, "What is the difference between the 'hidden Azal' and the Hidden Imám of Islam?" [7] Furthermore, I thought that his writings were just nonsense, except when he quoted from the Writings of the Báb. But I was confused and uncertain about these thoughts.

Then Jináb-i-Zayn brought me two Tablets of Bahá'u'lláh. I recognized a certain mysterious power and magic in every word. I fell in love with these Writings. Later, Ḥájí Siyyid Muḥammad Afnán, the uncle of the Báb, came to Iṣfahán and brought with him a precious gift—a copy of the Kitáb-i-Íqán, the Book of Certitude, which had been revealed in answer to his own questions. When I read this volume, I became a thousand times more attracted to Bahá'u'lláh, His Utterances, and His Writings. I would openly say that I regarded the Writings of Bahá'u'lláh as the greatest miracle ever performed. But some people were not happy with my views.

One of Azal's supporters told me, "Bahá'u'lláh wants

to take advantage of the prophecies of the Báb and claim the position of 'Him Whom God shall make manifest.' Therefore, he has imprisoned Azal. Sometimes he beats him and forces him to produce books which Bahá'u'lláh then publishes in his own name."

When he said these things I was amazed. I had never heard such nonsense. I protested that the Kitáb-i-Íqán was a matchless work, while the writings of Azal were neither significant nor well written. He claimed that the Íqán was written by Azal and that those writings which were attributed to him were not really his. This increased my amazement. However, since the conversation was friendly and confidential, I did not argue with him but kept the matter to myself.

I continued to transcribe the Bayán. But soon I became too well known in Iṣfahán, and my friends began to avoid me. Finally I was left alone and homeless.

There was a large, abandoned religious school where only a poor teacher conducted children's classes. I found lodging in a room in this old school. I had nothing with me but a copy of the Qur'án, the Bayán, the Kitáb-i-Íqán, and the Mat͟hnaví.[8] I prepared myself for four months of retreat.

The caretaker used to prepare food for me, and as long as I lived in that dilapidated place, I met no one and no one knew I was there. Gradually I began to realize that seclusion is a waste of one's life. I reminded myself that one's actions should be pleasing to God, but this could not be accomplished unless one was of service and guided the people to the right path of God, that is, to His new Manifestation. Therefore, I decided to leave Iṣfahán.

For more than six years I journeyed from town to town and from village to village, across the length and breadth of central Iran. Although I traveled under the most difficult circumstances, I was in a state of the utmost joy. Everywhere, I proclaimed the advent of the Báb and the Expected One Whom God would make manifest. On many occasions people attacked me, beat me, imprisoned me, and caused me unbearable suffering. Very often I was beaten more than I had appetite for.

On one occasion, when I had been beaten most severely and my body was covered with wounds, one of the members of the 'Alíyu'lláhí sect came to my rescue. These people have peculiar and exaggerated ideas concerning the rank and position of 'Alí, the cousin of the Prophet Muḥammad. This man offered me hospitality until my wounds were healed. When I regained enough strength, I resumed my journey.

I went to Shíráz and proceeded directly to the Ílkhání Mosque, where Mullá Ḥusayn and his friends had once taken lodging. While I was there, I met Ḥájí Siyyid Muḥammad Afnán (the uncle of the Báb) and some other believers. I found the friends in Shíráz to be wholeheartedly attracted to Bahá'u'lláh. There was no mention of Azal. Jináb-i-Afnán's [9] countenance was always beaming with joy and sweet smiles.

One of the friends, Siyyid 'Abdu'l-Raḥím, who was well versed in the Bayán, had extracted many verses with which he would prove that the One Who would be manifested could be none other than Bahá'u'lláh, and that Azal was only a name without a reality. That same siyyid related the following story:

"After the martyrdom of the Báb, when Azal had become famous, I traveled to Ṭihrán just to meet him. But I remembered that, when I was in Badasht, I had seen manifest reverence paid to Bahá'u'lláh by no less than Quddús and Ṭáhirih, and, as a matter of fact, by every person in that great conference.

"When I reached Ṭihrán, I met Bahá'u'lláh in the bazaar. At this time, His glory was hidden under a myriad veils of light. He approached me and asked me if I had come to see Azal. I answered affirmatively. I went, in His company, to His house. Once there, He asked for tea to be served. Azal brought the samovar, served the tea, and remained standing in the presence of Bahá'u'lláh. Bahá'u'lláh spoke to me and rivers of knowledge and wisdom flowed forth from His mouth. After drinking tea, He stood up, turned to Azal, and said, 'He has come to see you.' Then He went into the inner court of the house. Azal sat down. I bowed low before him to express my respect. Naturally, I expected him to speak to me, but he said nothing at all."

TO EARN MY LIVING, I would transcribe books for people. At times I became a doctor. At other times I wrote amulets and foretold the future. Sometimes I was an exorcist. By the grace of God, I was successful at whatever I attempted. The money I thus earned I divided in two parts: some to cover the bare necessities of my own life and the rest to feed the destitute. Some nights I had nothing but water.

In those days one often met men called dervishes, who spent their time, wealth, and energy trying to discover what they called "the elixir," a substance with which they would be able to change base metal into gold. They had many old manuscripts describing the process, and I was able to increase my income by copying some of these old books for them. They really believed that eventually they would be able to change mountains into masses of gold.

I am always astounded by the fact that the followers of the already established religions will deny whatever proof we offer them of the truth of the Message of God for this Day but will believe in all sorts of miracles performed not only by their own Prophets, but by mysterious forces emanating from the graves of some of their followers.

EVENTUALLY I made my way to Baghdád, traveling that great distance on foot. I traversed deserts and mountains, living very frugally. Although I endured many physical deprivations, I still remember, often and lovingly, the joy of those days. Sometimes I long for a moment of those intoxicating times.

I used to walk for several days before I would reach a village where I could rest to cure the blisters and regain strength to resume my journey. Some of the innkeepers were very hard. Either they would not allow me to enter or they would demand exorbitant prices. Nevertheless, I continued my long march toward the city of Baghdád.

I already knew that Jináb-i-Zayn was in Baghdád and that most of the friends did business in a marketplace called the Súqu'l-Ḥaráj. When I reached Baghdád, I immediately made for this market and with the help of friends sought Jináb-i-Zayn.

An uncle of mine, whom I had never seen, had decided to transfer his residence from Iran to the holy cities of Karbilá and Najaf. His name was Mírzá Muḥammad-i-Vakíl.[10] I did not know that he had become a believer. Through Jináb-i-Zayn we met each other. He took me to his house and showed me much kind hospitality. I later learned that among the more than eighty believers who had been imprisoned and exiled from Baghdád to

Mosul were my uncle and Jináb-i-Zayn. After some years my uncle returned to Baghdád, and Jináb-i-Zayn, on Bahá'u'lláh's instructions, made the Holy Land his home.

Ismu'lláh Munír[11] was in Baghdád when I arrived there. Munír was a great man adorned with all the heavenly virtues. I spent much of my time with this illumined and illustrious soul. A certain friend called Áqá Mírzá Javád also lived in that town. He had committed to memory the text of the entire Qayyúmu'l-Asmá', the Commentary on the Sura of Joseph written by the Báb. He used to recite it and explain the words of the Báb. He was faithful to Bahá'u'lláh and would not say anything about Azal.

After some time I returned to Shíráz by way of Baṣrih and Búshihr. In Shíráz I happened to meet Shujá'u'l-Mulk, one of the army chiefs who had fought against Vahíd in Nayríz. Though an enemy of the Cause, he confessed that Vahíd was the most erudite person of his time, particularly with regard to the Qur'án and its interpretation. He even went on to state that Vahíd and his followers had fought as courageously as the martyrs of Karbilá.[12]

I also met the treasurer of Prince Mihdí Qulí Mírzá, one of those who commanded the government forces in the Ṭabarsí upheavals.[13] He told me that there were three statements which he considered to be monstrous lies: "One, that I embraced this religion and then recanted my faith. Whoever says this lies when he claims that I converted and lies when he claims that I recanted. Two, that Mullá Ḥusayn fought with me and wounded me. Anyone whom Mullá Ḥusayn struck in battle died immediately. Three, that I fought with Mullá Ḥusayn face to face. Actually, he was facing away from me, and I shot him in the back and killed him."

In Ṭihrán I again met Jináb-i-Munír. Since he knew of my convictions and of my love for the Ancient Beauty,[14] he showed me a Tablet called the Súriy-i-Aṣḥáb, which had been revealed in his honor by Bahá'u'lláh. As I read this Tablet, I felt in every verse a fire of enthusiasm, and I could not control my feelings. So I turned to Jináb-i-Munír and asked him whether Siyyid Muḥammad [15] had deceived Azal, or Azal had deceived Siyyid Muḥammad, or whether the two of them had simply joined together in rebellion against Bahá'u'lláh. When Jináb-i-Munír heard these words he embraced me and kissed me and said, "The enemies of Bahá'u'lláh are united in one thing alone, and that is to join forces against Him. They deceive and mislead each other in order to oppose Him."

I was set on fire by reading the Súriy-i-Aṣḥáb. I felt such joy and spiritual exultation that even now, after fifty years, although I am getting older and all my senses are waning, the mere thought of those memorable moments sets my soul ablaze and ignites the lamp of my heart.

The Báb proclaimed the glad tidings of the advent of Bahá'u'lláh, and in the six years of His ministry He prepared the people perfectly, made the way clear, and planted the seeds of love and obedience to the Promised One in the hearts of the Bábís. Bahá'u'lláh served the

Bábí Faith and educated, protected, and nurtured the Bábís in such a way that eventually ninety-nine out of a hundred came to recognize in Him the fulfillment of all the promises of the Báb. Bahá'u'lláh sowed the seeds, provided them with the water they needed, protected them from the evil deeds of the enemies, attended them tenderly, and encouraged them to grow more vigorous each day. Therefore, when the hour decreed by God arrived and Bahá'u'lláh revealed His station, the true believers turned their hearts and souls to the Ancient Beauty and found no veil but light, and no hindrance but intense splendor.

Najaf-'Alí [16] was one of those true believers. At the time of his martyrdom he gave thanks and was heard to say, "We have found Bahá and we hasten to offer our lives as a sacrifice to Him. He is our ransom." He was so enkindled that he hastened to his death with the utmost joy and exultation. When the cup of martyrdom was brought to him and he saw it overflowing, he exclaimed, "There is a custom in our province. The bride is taken on horseback to the house of her future husband. When the bridegroom sees his bride approaching, he gives the owner of the horse sumptuous gifts such as costly clothes and gold coins." He then addressed the executioner, saying, "I have long stored these gold coins for this day—the day of my greatest happiness. Here they are! Take them!" Then he pulled out a sack of coins from his pocket and with intense joy offered it to his executioner.

Another believer, being taken to his death, asked the executioner, "Would you be so kind as to cut my vein first and give me time before the final blow?" The executioner, hoping that the old man would recant his faith, held his dagger to his victim's neck, making a wound. To his extreme surprise, he found the martyr holding his hands like a cup and filling them with his blood. The believer then cried out, "O people, be my witness! Here I testify to the truth of my faith with my own blood."

IT WAS NEAR Naw-Rúz when I made for Adrianople. On the way, I passed through Qazvín, where I went to the house of Mírzá Muḥammad-'Alí Kad-Khudá, who was one of the notables and dignitaries of the province. I met some of the friends there. My host related to me the following:

"I was a dervish and the follower of a mystic leader called Mírzá Kúchik-i-Shírází. He knew Ṭáhirih and had extraordinary praise for her knowledge, audacity, faith, and spiritual power. Because of this I once asked my mystic leader, 'What do you think of the Báb's claim?' to which he retorted, 'The Báb has written a unique and unsurpassed commentary on the Sura of Kawthar. Should He lay down His pen, no one of the past or present would ever dare to pick it up. But, unfortunately, He has not studied under or served any of the mystic leaders.'

"This answer made me sad and forced me to contemplate the words he had spoken. I repeated to myself again and again, 'He says that no one can ever dare to pick up His pen, yet He must be schooled and trained by a mystic leader like himself. How strange!' As a matter of fact, his answer drew me to the Báb and I embraced His Faith."

In Zanján I met 'Abá Basír, Siyyid Ashraf, and Mullá Ibráhím.

Mullá Ibráhím was from a village near Iṣfahán. This simple-hearted and innocent man had suffered so much in his own village that he was forced to forsake his home, friends, and relatives and seek refuge and shelter in this far-off district of Iran.

Before he left his village he had been in prison. As was the case in those days, the jailer constantly demanded bribes from the prisoners in exchange for providing them with the barest essentials of life. Mullá Ibráhím told the jailers that he had no money but was willing to work. So he earned his frugal living as a laborer in the prison. After he was released from prison, he went to his village to gather a little money from the sale of his house and property, but he learned that his relatives had taken everything. In order to find shelter and security, he left home, village, and relatives for a distant province in the north.

His joy was to work, earn a little money, spend very little on himself, and give the rest to the poor. He agreed to go with me on pilgrimage to Adrianople and promised to meet me in Tabríz. On his way there, two men clad as dervishes joined him, pretending to be believers on their way to Adrianople. They won his confidence; then they stole what little money he had and ran away. He reached Tabríz empty-handed but determined to go on with me despite his misfortune.

Now, on my way to Adrianople, many thoughts passed through my mind. In my childhood I had learned a tradition about how a man shall meet his Lord on the Day of Judgment. According to this tradition, those who are honored with meeting their Lord on this Day will find themselves intoxicated with the wine of paradise and will experience such joy as is beyond description. I knew that the true meaning of this tradition was to attain the presence of the Manifestation of God and that such a meeting would be as heaven on earth. I was fond of this tradition, and by the grace of God I was permitted to discover for myself that it was true.

I also had a conversation with Ḥájí Siyyid Javád-i-Karbilá'í. This great man had the honor of meeting and studying with Shaykh Aḥmad and Siyyid Káẓim. He became one of the early believers in the Báb, and he embraced the Faith of Bahá'u'lláh and lived near Him during the Baghdád period. The Báb appointed him one of the Mirrors of the Dispensation of the Bayán. A follower of Azal once asked Siyyid Javád, in the presence of others, to describe the countenance of the Báb. He immediately said, "He was unsurpassed in beauty and sweetness. Have you heard of the beauty of Joseph? [17] This is what I mean." Fearing that his answer might be taken to mean that he was a follower of Azal, I asked him about Bahá'u'lláh, and he immediately replied, "Know with certainty that if anyone, friend or enemy, claims to have looked directly into His eyes, he is a liar. I tested this again and again but all my attempts to look at Him were in vain. Sometimes the friends were so carried away in His presence that, in their bewilderment, they would forget the world within and without. Can one fix one's gaze upon the sun?"

During the seven months I stayed in Adrianople, I came to realize what those words of Ḥájí Siyyid Javád meant. Fifteen years after that, I went to 'Akká to visit Bahá'u'lláh. Often I desired to know what color of táj he wore, and yet I forgot to think of it every time I was in His presence. One day, He was having His midday meal in a small room at the Garden of Riḍván. Some of the friends were inside, while others were standing in rows outside. From behind the crowd of believers, at last I could glimpse the marvelous táj on his head. Its color was green.

What happened in my soul and heart while I was with Him was an inner and mysterious experience beyond the scope of my words to describe. One of the mullás of Iṣfahán once asked me, "What did you see when you were in His presence?"

I said, "I had expected to see all sorts of miracles. I also had several questions that I wanted to ask. But when I attained His presence all this became unimportant. I had found the pure water which quenches thirst and gives true life."

The mullá asked, "What did you see?"

"I saw the form of a human being," I replied. "But His every step and movement was like a miracle to me. I saw *Him* and my eyes could take in nothing else, for He is different from all others in His bearing and in His manner. He is unique by Himself. No one in the world can ever be compared to Him. He is the One Whom the Qur'án has declared to have neither father nor son." [18]

"But Bahá'u'lláh's father was well known!" the man replied. And his son, 'Abbás Effendi, is renowned for his perfections!"

"I saw neither father nor son," was my response.

"Bahá'u'lláh alone is the Source of God's Revelation. He is the One Who 'begetteth not, nor is He begotten.' If you stand before a mirror and speak your name, your image will do likewise, but it is an illusion." The clergyman was pleased with my answer and asked me more about the Faith.

ONE OF THE most famous merchants of Qazvín was Ḥájí Muḥammad Báqir. Not only was he well known as a merchant, but he was also prominent in his service to the Cause, a service which was much appreciated by all the believers. Once he sent a letter to Bahá'u'lláh asking Him to bestow upon him the bounty of wealth so that he could serve the Cause with greater capacity. Bahá'u'lláh answered that the doors of wealth would be opened to him from all sides, but he must be ever vigilant lest material prosperity become a veil between him and his Creator.

Bahá'u'lláh also said to those in His presence at the time that Muḥammad Báqir would soon be drowned in wealth, but material success would close his eyes to the realities of life to such a degree that he would turn his back on the Cause and even deny God. But he would suffer tremendous losses and would return to his Lord in repentance. Because of his repentance, God would change his losses into ample profits to such an extent as to enable him to become the leading merchant in Tabríz and Constantinople. This time he would become even more proud and would again ignore the Faith, and then his wealth would be gone forever. He would no longer be able to trade and would become helpless. He would then return in repentance once more and remain poor but content. In this state, he would serve the Cause and achieve great success in his service to God. At the end of His wondrous and ominous statement, Bahá'u'lláh addressed me and advised that I should remember all the events as they unfolded.

After some time, Muḥammad Báqir's brother was arrested and thrown into prison because of his Faith. Muḥammad Báqir paid a large sum of money to obtain his brother's release. After that, Muḥammad Báqir made his way to Constantinople. Upon his arrival, he recanted his faith and approached the court of the sultan and the Persian ambassador, begging them to consider him a true Muslim.

Bahá'u'lláh immediately remarked that this was the starting point of the chain of events he had described before.

I then went to Constantinople, where I stayed fourteen months. There I learned that Muḥammad Báqir had purchased great quantities of cotton. All of a sudden, the price of cotton dropped so low that our friend lost his wealth and became submerged in debt. In this deplorable condition, he again remembered his Lord and wrote a letter to Bahá'u'lláh in which he repented and begged Him to come to his aid. Bahá'u'lláh replied, assuring him that he would regain his wealth.

When I was in Egypt I learned that the price of cotton had risen sharply. Muḥammad Báqir's wealth grew to ten times more than ever before. Although he had been tested once, he fell a second time into the trap of greed and failed to know his Lord and Provider. Bahá'u'lláh wrote him again and alerted him to the danger of material temptation. He exhorted him to remain steadfast in the Path of God and grateful for His bounties. But once more Muḥammad Báqir ignored God and remained heedless.

When after many years I found him again in Tabríz,

he told me, "After I received the Tablet, it seemed to me that even the nails and curtains on the walls of my room had ears to hearken and obey. One by one, all of my possessions slipped quietly from me. I was reduced to poverty and was forced to leave Constantinople for Tabríz where I live in this house, which belongs to my wife, and wear clothes that are made by my children."

AZAL WROTE a letter to the governor of Adrianople complaining about Bahá'u'lláh. He had no aim in doing so except to heap calumny on Bahá'u'lláh and attempt to place Him in an untenable position. The governor, who knew Bahá'u'lláh, took Azal's letter to His house and sought His instructions. The Ancient Beauty replied, "Ask him to come and see Me. If he comes, then whatever he says is right."

The governor asked Azal to go to the house where he could meet Bahá'u'lláh. To this simple request Azal answered, "We do not go to each other's houses, and He will not come to the governor's house." Eventually the Great Mosque of Sultan Salím was chosen as the meeting place for Bahá'u'lláh and Azal.

On a Friday morning, Bahá'u'lláh started out for the mosque. The people, anticipating His approach, thronged the way between His house and the mosque. All stood in reverence and awe to receive His blessing, hoping for even one glimpse of Him. The street was so full of people that all other travel was stopped. The people in the crowd spontaneously raised their voices in salutation and praise. They tried to approach Him, and some prostrated themselves in His path, hoping to kiss His feet. With great joy and respect for

Bahá'u'lláh, they elbowed one another and made way for Him to pass through. In response to all these reverent salutations, Bahá'u'lláh raised His hand again and again and pronounced words of greeting: "Marḥabá! Marḥabá! Báriku'lláh fíkum." ("Greetings! Greetings! May God bless you all.")

As soon as He entered the mosque, the preacher who was addressing the immense congregation from his high pulpit stopped the sermon and fell silent—either by choice or because he forgot what he had to say. Bahá'u'lláh took His seat and asked the man to continue. Time passed and everyone expected Azal to arrive also, but to their great surprise he never appeared.

There are dervishes who gather together, usually on Friday mornings, to sing the poems of the Mat͟hnaví, and to mention the names of God, repeating, "He is God! O God!" To the rhythm of this chant and the sound of music and drums, the worshipers sing and sing, dance and dance, whirl and whirl, gradually increasing their speed until they become intoxicated with the mention of God and are attracted to Him, and His greatness and majesty. On that Friday morning, when Bahá'u'lláh left the mosque to return to His house, He heard the dervishes singing, and He said to His companions, "Mawlaná [19] needs a visit from Us." The governor, his officials, and the notables of the town, finding this a great and unique opportunity, followed Bahá'u'lláh.

The mayor, S͟hayk͟hu'l-Islám, and the 'ulamá kept a distance of at least five paces behind Him. Every now and then Bahá'u'lláh would stop and ask them to approach, but they remained where they were, saluting Him in their fashion by placing their hands on their chests and bowing their heads in utter respect and reverence. In this order, they followed Bahá'u'lláh into the takyih.[20] The dervishes were in the midst of their shouting and rapid whirling, and the music was louder than ever. But when Bahá'u'lláh entered the takyih, the proceedings came to a stop and all fell absolutely silent. Bahá'u'lláh sat down and very graciously motioned to His companions to take a seat where they could; then He allowed the dervishes to resume their activities.

The night after that memorable day, I had the honor of being in His presence. Bahá'u'lláh said that when He entered the mosque the preacher forgot his sermon; and when He entered the takyih the dervishes stopped, awestruck, and were unable to continue singing and whirling. As the people of the world are brought up and trained in vain imaginings, they take such events as miracles, but God and His Prophets are in realms beyond man's reach and comprehension.

In Adrianople, as well as in the Holy Land, I heard Him tell us about the events of His own life. He often remarked that should the people ponder the life of the Báb—His captivity, imprisonment, and martyrdom, and His Writings—they would surely realize what a gift He gave to the world, that throughout such an eventful life the hand of God remained forever far above the understanding and reach of man.

Pondering His life, captivity, and exiles, one would surely come to realize that enemies of the Faith, their rulers, potentates, and kings, despite their well-equipped soldiers, well-organized plans, and cunning stratagems, were invariably turned into an army which caused the progress, proclamation, and solidarity of the Faith of God.

In the early days of the Faith in Iṣfahán, when I first became acquainted with the beautiful Writings of the Báb, I was captured by their power and majesty. The words were like a string of pearls. The proofs and arguments of the friends were so overwhelming that I felt no one could ever deny their truth. But when I was alone I would become the target of suspicions, vain imaginings, and evil whisperings. All that I had read and learned previously would then come before me. The purgatory implied in all the Books of God surrounded me. To overcome this terrible period of testing was indeed difficult. Only God knows of my anguish and the many hours I wept. I passed many a sleepless night when rest and comfort abandoned me. Some days I concentrated so much on my own spiritual dilemma that I forgot to eat. Many a time I pushed away all evil thoughts and became a firm believer, but with the slightest negative thought I would once again retreat and almost deny my newfound belief.

Then, one night, I dreamed that a town crier appeared in the bazaar of Iṣfahán, announcing the advent of the Prophet Muḥammad and proclaiming that whoever wished to meet Him could go to a certain house and attain His presence. He said that a glimpse of His countenance was even more worthy than service in this world and the world to come. On hearing this, I hastened to the house wherein the Prophet Muḥammad was said to be, and, having entered, I prostrated myself at His feet. He lifted me up with the utmost love, and then He addressed me, saying, "One may claim that he has come here only for the sake of God, and has attained the presence of his Lord, only when he has stood firm against a world of enemies who have drawn their swords against him because he has embraced this Cause. Otherwise, he cannot say that his motive was to find God."

I awoke and found myself in a state of joy and certitude. At that moment I came to understand the mystery of suffering and the reason why the followers of all the Prophets have suffered. I rebuked myself time and again, and said, "I had read all those heavenly utterances of the Báb, yet I had to reach the state of belief and certitude through a dream."

Fourteen years later, I found myself in Adrianople, where I stayed for about seven months. One night, when I was in the tearoom with Áqá Muḥammad-Qulí, I felt a longing to be in the presence of Bahá'u'lláh, even for a short while. I had not the courage to ask for such an audience since it was very late. Suddenly, 'Abdu'l-Bahá opened the door and asked me to follow Him. Having left the room, I found Bahá'u'lláh walking on the roofed area of the house. Some of the friends were standing and listening to His utterances.

Then I was admitted to the presence of the Ancient Beauty. I prostrated myself at His feet. He picked me up with love and gentleness and said, "One may claim that he has come here only for the sake of God, and has attained the presence of his Lord, only when he has stood firm against a world of enemies who have drawn their swords against him because he has embraced this Cause."

As I write this I have not the slightest intention of relating a miracle, but only wish to state the facts as they occurred. We cannot comprehend such confirmations from the Chosen Ones of God. The faculty of man's understanding may be likened to a man who is lame or paralyzed, while the minds of the Prophets of God move as swiftly as lightning through the firmament. How could these two forces ever come together?

THAT EVENING there was talk of my leaving Adrianople. Bahá'u'lláh sent a message to find out about my plans—whether I desired to stay or depart, and if the latter, when and to where. I hastened to the beloved Master, 'Abdu'l-Bahá, and begged Him, "Please do not abandon me to myself. Do not ask me about my desire, plan, or will. Let His will be done. Let Him order me to go and confirm me to do whatever He desires. I am homeless, of simple needs, and have no one who depends upon me." My plea was accepted and His instructions were conveyed to me that I should take up residence in Constantinople with the responsibility to receive Tablets and letters and dispatch them to their destinations, and also to help the friends on their way to and from pilgrimage in Adrianople.

My companion in Constantinople was Mírzá Ḥusayn, and my joy and consolation was to have in my possession the Tablets I had brought in the handwriting of the Master and Mírzá Músá (Áqáy-i-Kalím).[21] What a joyful time was ours!

We had the honor of meeting the believers, receiving Tablets, dispatching them regularly to the friends, and preparing those things which were required for the household in Adrianople. I also had an opportunity to meet the pilgrims on their way to Adrianople. They had to remain a few days in Constantinople making preparations for the journey or seeking permission from Bahá'u'lláh for pilgrimage. They also stayed a few days on their way back.

Jináb-i-Kalím used to write regularly and keep us in touch with the glorious tidings from the presence of Bahá'u'lláh. And Áqá Muḥammad-'Alí would write concerning the purchase of things required for the House in Adrianople. Once he ordered some tea. I purchased some and sent it, but he was not satisfied with its quality and wrote me a very gentle letter pointing out that I should pay more attention because such goods were to be used by the Holy Family. Being young, haughty, and proud, I took offense at this small piece of kindly advice. In a state of bitterness I wrote an answer which was not courteous and, indeed, not even worthy of a believer.

A little time passed, and I received a Tablet from Bahá'u'lláh assuring me that all my services had been graciously accepted and expressing His approval and pleasure. When I read this Tablet, I realized that the letter I had written had been a grave mistake. Having lived seven months in His presence, I had come to know that this Supreme Manifestation of God chastises the souls of sinners with the scourge of love and compassion, for their own edification. He conceals our mistakes and forgives us so that the wrongdoers will receive divine education. In addition to that, His forgiving and merciful attitude to the people shows them by example the right path to tolerance and servitude.

When, through this bountiful attitude, I was awakened and came to realize what an impolite letter I had written to one of the servants of the Household, I turned to God, wept, and prayed fervently for forgiveness. I was in a deep state of distress and dismay. Again, I turned to 'Abdu'l-Bahá for help. I implored the Master to intervene and ask forgiveness for me. Then instructions came that I should go to Egypt. This assured me that I had been honored with the garment of pardon and mercy. Before departing, I went to Adrianople on another pilgrimage. During the last moment of my audience with Bahá'u'lláh, He assured me that I would attain His presence again.

Before I reached the continent of Africa, the Persians in Constantinople had written to those in Egypt warning them about the arrival of "the Gabriel of the Bábís." This made many of them hasten to my place of residence to behold such an unusual creature—a Bábí. Some came in and inquired, "Why did you abandon Muḥammad, the Seal of the Prophets? Why did you withdraw your hand from the hem of the garment of our innocent Imáms? Why did you exclude yourselves from the Muslim community?"

I was at a loss for what to say or do! I had been instructed to be cautious and even to remain unknown. Now, if I hid myself and my faith, and did not utter a word in answer to these questions, they would accuse me of being a coward or of being ashamed of my beliefs. I knew there would be no end to such questions, but I felt that I needed to give some response so they would not consider the followers of the Faith ignorant or unfaithful. Therefore, I answered them.

"We are not here to cause confusion or dissension," I said. "Will you not show some kindness and let us discuss things on the basis of mutual understanding and good will? Let us fix our sole aim on finding out the truth.

"All that you have said so far consists of accusations and slander against us and has no basis at all. We believe wholeheartedly that the Qu'rán is the Book of God, that obedience to it is compulsory, and that its verses are a guide to the path of truth. It is in this Book that we find the story in which a man from the family of Pharaoh, who was a believer and concealed his faith, said, 'Will ye slay a man because he saith my Lord is God, when

He hath already come to you with signs from your Lord? If he be a liar, on him will be his lie, but if he be a man of truth, part of what he threatened will fall upon you. In truth God guideth not him who is a transgressor, a liar.'

"Surely you have heard of a certain notable from the lineage of the Prophet Muḥammad. Though this Siyyid was saintly in every aspect of His life and guided the people to God and His Prophets, He was severely persecuted, exiled, imprisoned, and finally put to death by a firing squad of many soldiers. You also have heard of thousands who followed His footsteps to persecution and martyrdom. Those who quaffed the cup of suffering and ignominious death were not of the ordinary people. There were among them the erudite, the chief clergy of the Islamic faith, philosophers, saints, mystic leaders, siyyids, and chieftains. Now the least that is incumbent upon the Muslims is to follow the example of that man from the family of Pharaoh and leave me in peace."

They said, "What shall we do? We said exactly what our religious leaders told us to say. They have even forbidden us to approach you, contact you, or talk to you."

I told them, "Have you ever heard or read anywhere that when a Prophet manifested Himself, the clergy told Him, 'You are welcome'? The Prophet Muḥammad, Jesus Christ, Moses, and the others have been the targets of the most cruel accusations heaped upon them by the most learned of their times. The Imám Ḥusayn was put to death by a decree signed and sealed by the most prominent religious dignitaries of his era. As for me, I do not even consider myself as equal to the dust of the footsteps of the least of Their lovers. I am not here to teach; I do not think of myself as worthy of such an exalted position."

This discussion proved at least to be a good introduction. For three days the people remained hostile. But after that, they became friendly toward me. They even invited me into their houses. Ḥájí Mírzá Javád-i-Shírází was one of them and considered by all to be the most notable and honored of the Persian merchants. He had seen the Báb in Shíráz and was full of admiration and reverence for Him. He often praised Him by saying that the Báb was unsurpassed in beauty, spirituality, and courtesy. There was no one equal to Him in nobility, accomplishments, and saintly qualities. He remained as One alone, unique in the age in which He lived.

Another one was Ḥájí Muḥammad-Ḥasan-i-Kázirúní. He eventually embraced the Faith, but did not reveal it to anyone. Ḥájí Muḥammad Rafí'á was also a well-known individual, famous for his truthfulness and laudable traits of character and manners.

Ḥájí Abu'l-Qásim-i-Shírází often used to come and meet me, but always in secret. The reason he gave for this was that he could not trust the friendship of his compatriots. But the time came when he could no longer hide his faith. He was seventy and became so ignited with the fire of certitude that he burned away all the veils separating him from his Beloved. He was totally transformed; that is to say, his fear was changed into audacity. He had been alone, but now he brought his family from Shíráz. He manifested such praiseworthy traits of character that his friends were astonished. He often said, "Wealth and riches are good, but only when they are spent in the path of the Cause of God. Otherwise they will cause misery and the loss of one's own soul."

He decided to go and behold the Countenance of the Ancient Beauty, but he had to get traveling documents from the Persian ambassador in Constantinople. It was extremely difficult, especially when they discovered that the applicant's intention was to go to Adrianople. He had to pay the ambassador a large sum of money, but he persevered and finally the difficulties were removed.

When he returned from his pilgrimage, he was utterly a new creation. Now he was steadfast in the Cause and could stand alone against the whole world. He was indeed like an unshakable mountain which had changed into a flowing river. His knowledge, love, and enthusiasm became exemplary. He could no longer remain silent. The stories of his pilgrimage were his favorite subject, and he always related them with the same joy and vigor.

It is worthwhile pondering the fact that he was seventy years old, and his thoughts, manners, and customs were deeply ingrained. It is a well-known saying that "when a man becomes old, two characteristics will be reinvigorated in him—greed and ambition." Yes, he became greedy, but to spend all that he had in the path of the propagation of the Cause. He also grew young in his hopes and ambitions, but these ambitions were to spread the Word of God.

THE PERSIAN CONSUL advised many people to associate with me and even to pretend that they were believers. Ḥusayn Hakkak and Mírzá Ṣafá were among them. They would come to my room, and to win my confidence they would speak very highly of the Faith. Mírzá Ṣafá claimed that he had seen the Báb in Búshihr where he had recognized in Him the signs of the exalted station destined for Him. Afterwards I learned that these two had been the special agents of the consul sent to find out the names and addresses of all the believers in Egypt.

The day approached when all Shí'ih Muslims would commemorate the martyrdom of the Imám 'Alí. The consul invited me to come to his house on this especially holy night. He told me that all the Persians in the city would be busy that night with prayers and that he would send home the servants of his household. "My house will be empty, and we will be alone to discuss whatever we wish," he explained.

A certain man, who was an old friend of mine, used to meet me very often. He was a man of no religion and, as a matter of fact, was against all of the Prophets. When I received the consul's invitation, he urged me not to accept, explaining that it was surely a device by which the consul could get me under his flag, in his office, and then arrest me and make me a prisoner. If this happened, he explained, the Egyptian government would not be able to protest. Even if they came to my aid, the consul would level accusations against me and slander me, and none of these charges would be challenged by anyone. He also reminded me that I had no one to stand on my side or to shield or defend me against such evil plots. I listened carefully to him, but I decided to accept the invitation because refusal would indicate weakness and fear, which are not worthy attributes for the followers of this great Faith.

I was reassured by remembering parts of the Tablets revealed by Bahá'u'lláh in my honor. In them He exhorted me to remember His exile, imprisonment, and hardship and to follow in His footsteps on the path of salvation. The believers should accept calamities and never be despondent in the face of persecution, but trust their Lord and remain happy, joyous, and steadfast as a mountain.

As I recalled the statements in my own Tablets, I became sure that imprisonment awaited me. Nevertheless, I went to the house of the consul at the appointed hour along with Mírzá Ḥusayn-i-Shírází and Darvísh Ḥasan. At first we behaved as Muslims, observing all the outward customs of Islám. But when the time came for the evening prayer, we demurred, saying, "Congregational prayer is forbidden, except for the dead." This led to a discussion of the Faith, and we spent the whole evening discussing the proofs of this Revelation. We even recited one of the Tablets of Bahá'u'lláh and related the sufferings of the heroes and martyrs of the Faith. The consul appeared to be impressed and even convinced.

Dawn was approaching when the consul retired. One of the servants came to convey our host's message that we should go home. This message astounded us because at first the consul had treated us very kindly, but now, at the hour of our departure, he rudely ordered us out of his house, not even having the manners to take leave of his guests. We left his house with a sense of foreboding. The consul had sent some people to carry lamps ahead of us to light the way through the dark and narrow lanes of the town. As we were treading the path toward my home, I discovered that, every few steps, more men joined our company. As I was thinking over this strange situation, we suddenly found ourselves surrounded by at least forty people who were indeed as devouring wolves.

We were dragged to the prison, where they robbed us of our clothing and placed all of us in chains and fetters, beating us with whatever was in their hands and cursing in the most horrible way. This continued until morning, when they closed the doors of the prison and went away. I was content, but my companions were rather despondent. I did what I could to raise their spirits.

The prison door remained closed to us the whole day. In the evening it opened, and we were allowed to go out for food and to say our prayers. At this time we learned that they had gone to my room and stolen all my possessions—clothes, books, works of calligraphy, and other precious articles. They gave me some old clothes, and when I said that the clothes did not belong to me, they became wild once again and began to torment us even more than before. Finally, they gave us a paper to sign. It was a receipt they had written explaining that, except for our books, all our belongings had been returned to us. We were forced to sign and seal this false document. They particularly mentioned the names of certain books and Tablets, because they planned to show the receipt to the Egyptian authorities and tell them that we were in possession of strange and dangerous writings.

They grudged no effort to invent all sorts of false reports against us for submission to the Egyptian rulers, and their poisonous slander reached the members of the court. They represented themselves as the most sincere friends and well-wishers of the khedive [22] and stated that they were in fact protecting the Egyptians from the onslaught of the Bábís. They reported that the Bábís had made an attempt on the life of the shah of Iran [23] and, having failed there, had dared to come to Egypt. The sovereign and the citizenry must be protected against such people, they argued, as they are sure to have friends and collaborators amongst the people of Egypt, Turkey, and Iran.

The khedive, who had no son to succeed him, became very fearful, and it was natural for him to be so under the circumstances. Unfortunately, we were not in a position to defend ourselves against these false accusations. We tried to explain that we were Bahá'ís and not Bábís, and that Bahá'ís are loyal and obedient to their government. But we were not even allowed to open our mouths to utter a word in our own defense.

For more than fifty years during the reign of Náṣiri'd-Dín Sháh, the courtiers and officials of his government in Egypt had nothing better to do than to make false reports against us to the sovereign. They even untruthfully told him that they had discovered caches of arms and equipment in the houses of the "Bábís."

A night came when I was taken to the consul's chambers. The consul and an Egyptian officer were seated, and a group of jailers stood by. I observed also that there was a large group of people in chains. The consul suddenly became furious and, pointing his finger at me, shouted, "All of the trouble has been caused by this man, their Gabriel and their Prophet!" No sooner were these words uttered than some men came and seized me, tied my hands behind my back, and put a chain around my neck. This accusation had the desired effect on the khedive of Egypt, who immediately ordered the consul to arrest anyone belonging to this religion.

It did not take the consul long to arrest some three hundred people. We learned that he even arrested a few Egyptian subjects. Ḥájí Abu'l-Qásim was arrested, and when they brought the chain to be placed on his neck, he picked it up, kissed it, and, putting it around his neck, uttered the words, "Bismi'lláhi'l-Bahíyyi'l-Abhá!" ("In the name of God, the Glory of the All-Glorious!")

The consul, under the pretext of persecuting the Bábís, had planned to collect large sums of money in bribes. My cell in the consulate was adjacent to a large room where these three hundred people were imprisoned—Jews and Christians and Muslims. In order to free themselves from the tortures of imprisonment, these victims had to offer him money. Thus an increasing flow of income found its way into the pocket of the consul. Each prisoner who was to be freed had to come to my cell, curse me, spit in my face, beat me, and abuse all of the Holy Ones of our Faith. This action would be taken as proof that the prisoner had not been, or was no longer, a Bábí. But, as previously mentioned, they had to pay large sums of money as well. Some of these victims were ashamed and would not even look upon my face. Their tormentors forced them to look into my eyes and do whatever they were ordered to do.

During the forty-five days I spent in that jail, we suffered as in hell because of the consul's staff and servants. But my soul was in a state of the utmost joy. Had it not been for this sense of inner tranquillity and composure, I could never have endured the savage acts, profane oaths, and the blasphemous remarks of these people.

I was very happy in prison. The only exception was in the early hours of the day, when the cruel persecutors would come to our room to beat, curse, and abuse us. This was the worst part of our daily life in prison.

One night the consul had invited some of the Persian dignitaries and some people from the Egyptian aristocracy to his home. The consul ordered that I should be taken in chains to that banquet. When I entered, it reminded me of the captivity of the Imám Ḥusayn's family and their arrival at the great gathering in the house of the governor of Kufih.

Before the consul could speak, I sat down and addressed him, saying, "Throughout the history of all religions, the Chosen Ones of God have been persecuted, chained, and forced to endure great hardships. It is a well-known saying that calamities are for the friends of God, and those who deny Him always follow the path of cruelty and injustice. Please ask all these people who are gathered here tonight what we have done that we must be subjected to so much humiliation and injustice. Remember the exhortation in the Qur'án which states that even if an evildoer brings you a message, it is your duty to investigate. What religion sanctions the type of treatment we have received from you? You only listen to those who accuse and never give the victims an opportunity to open their mouths and explain their case." I spoke with such strength and authority that the consul ordered the jailers to take me back to my cell.

ONE TIME, a group of Persians arrived who were on their way to Mecca. To show them how strong a person he was and how he protected and served his religion and country, the consul brought all the pilgrims to my prison cell. The moment he entered, he began to beat me with his cane. Then he said, "Tell the truth. What is your name?"

"Ḥaydar-'Alí," I said.

"No!" he protested. "You have other names. You have been called 'The Gabriel of the Bábís,' 'The Amanuensis,' and 'The First Imám.' "

"I have never said this," I responded. "Someone has accused me of these things."

"Yes," he said.

"Well, his name must be Satan," I immediately replied, "because anyone who carries false reports and instigates people to act unjustly is none other than Satan. He always comes to people in such a way that they will not know him."

He hit me again and said, "Are you so presumptuous as to vilify the ambassador himself?"

They went out and brought back a man who accused

me of theft. He demanded that I return to him the belongings of his brother. When he mentioned the name of his brother, I said that I did not know him. While we were arguing, all the others went out, leaving only the man and myself. No sooner were we alone than he embraced me and kissed me, saying, "I am 'Abdu'lláh from Najafábád. I was in His presence. Now I am in Egypt on my way to Mecca. I heard about your imprisonment. Knowing that they have confiscated all your belongings, I had a little money and thought of bringing it to you." He gave me the money and continued, "I couldn't come into the prison to meet you unless I had some excuse. Therefore, I told the consul that his prisoner had the belongings of my brother. Now, whatever happens, I will be most grateful, even if he keeps me here with you in this prison cell. If he allows me to go, I will also be grateful to my Lord."

This same 'Abdu'lláh made his way to Jiddih where he met Ḥájí Mírzá Ṣafá. There, he became the servant of this mystic leader. Some of the Persians knew 'Abdu'lláh and were extremely surprised that a man who was a religious leader had employed such a well-known Bábí as his close and trusted servant. The following conversation took place between Mírzá Ṣafá and 'Abdu'lláh:

"I heard that you have been to Adrianople?"

"Should I have any shortcomings or show any disloyalty in my services to you, you have every right to consider me a sinner and worthy of chastisement. But you have not employed my conscience. Yes, it is true that I had the honor of making a pilgrimage to His presence in Adrianople."

"What did you see there?"

"All that I had heard about the past religions and the Prophets of God, I beheld in Him and in His Manifestation."

"How is it that you saw such signs while the learned,

the philosophers, and the mystic leaders have not seen such things?"

"It was the same in the days of the Prophet Muḥammad. The learned orators and philosophers denied Him, but the illiterate, the peddlers, and the slaves embraced His Faith."

"Bravo! You answer well."

After saying this, he gave 'Abdu'lláh his wages and some extra money, recommending to him that he go from Jiddih to Egypt, rather than to the resting place of the Prophet in the city of Medina. 'Abdu'lláh thought things over and said to himself, "I have endured hardships, and now I am here where the feet of the Prophet Muḥammad have trodden and where I can behold the sights seen by His own eyes. Why should I deprive myself of all these bounties?"

He was then determined to experience the full pilgrimage, and in Medina he once again met Mírzá Ṣafá, who remonstrated, "I told you to go to Egypt and not to come to Medina!"

"To pay homage to the Shrine of the Prophet Muḥammad is an act of worship and more important than obedience to you," 'Abdu'lláh responded.

"I want you to be in my employment again. You are an honest person, but at the same time I would like to give you some advice. Wise men never tread those paths on which they are perpetually confronted with many hardships, or on such roads where they are constantly faced with danger. They choose the highways that are well kept and secure, and along which are located many villages and towns. The path you have chosen for yourself will become, in time, a wonderful highway—but only after two hundred years or so. Now there are many dangers on it. You must avoid them."

"It is absolutely true. But you must know that people like me must travel these dangerous roads and undergo difficulties and deprivation to pave the way for people like you."

"How is it that you are so quick to answer and are so brave and daring in your response?" said Mírzá Ṣafá.

"In the Qur'án the Prophet Muḥammad has clearly said that those who long for death are always truthful. In order to tell the truth, no one requires meditation or careful thought, nor is the truthful man hesitant."

A GROUP OF US were entrusted to the Egyptian officers to be taken to an unknown destination. One of the friends in chains became so excited and happy that he recited a poem which says:

Against Thy Will not one complains,
Lions are not ashamed of chains.

When the people heard us reciting joyous poems as a sign of faith and steadfastness, some burst into tears and others into laughter. We were conducted to another prison, where the chains were taken from our wrists and necks. We spent the night there.

The next morning our fellow prisoners asked us what charges had been brought against us. We said that we did not know what the Persian consul had accused us of.

"Have you killed anyone?" they asked. "This prison is only for murderers and assassins."

We were not accused of murder, however. The charges against us were that we had abandoned Islam and created a new religion. So the next day I was able to write a petition in Arabic to the Egyptian officer in charge of the prison. In it I argued: "The most basic principles of justice require that one should serve the sentence for the crime of which he is accused. The Persian consul, because of his personal animosity toward us, has accused us of establishing a new religion and discarding the laws of Islam. Yet, we are in a prison for murderers.

"Not everyone can be accused of establishing a new religion. Anyone so accused must at least be learned and resourceful and respected by many people. To imprison us with murderers is most unjust."

The officer, fearing that we might lead the other prisoners astray, decided to move us to separate quarters. Our new room had carpets and a few other comforts, but the other prisoners were not allowed to speak to us.

A few days later, the consul came to the prison and saw our new quarters. We knew that from then on the conditions would be altered for the worse; and it was true.

Eight nights passed. On the ninth, shortly after midnight when all were asleep, soldiers came to our cell again, tied our hands behind our backs, and chained us all in one row. My hands were so tightly bound and so severely damaged that I felt the effects of those ropes for the rest of my life. Fifty soldiers, well armed and well equipped, took us on a stony road covered with thorns and thistles. Being ill and not sufficiently fed, we found walking very painful.

As we were going down the road, the soldiers fell into conversation with us. Gradually they realized that we were not violent prisoners and could not be any match for fifty soldiers. They asked us what we had done and we told them the truth. They began to feel pity for us. My hands were swollen and caused me much pain. First they released my hands, and then they became so kind and gentle that they even allowed us to ride horses in turn.

When we approached the famous prison of Famul-Baḥr, the soldiers again put us all in chains. They kept us outside the town and sent word to the governor, who specified our prison cell and ordered that we must be manacled together on one chain. He also emphasized that the prison cell must be dark and the doors should be bolted and locked. A hole was made in the door of our cell. The chain was stretched through this hole and was held firmly in the hands of the guards outside.

The day was almost as dark as the night, and when evening came no one gave us so much as a candle. We decided to chant the Tablet of Náqús, which had been revealed by Bahá'u'lláh for the celebration of the night on which the Báb had declared His mission. We were eight prisoners and our voices united in chanting the verses. When the soldiers heard this, they came in with a lamp for us. They thought that we were dervishes and that we were chanting something which contained the mention of God. This attracted their kindness toward us. Thereafter, the soldiers kept the doors of our cell open during the day and unchained us all.

IT WAS NOT LONG before officers, notables, merchants, and people of each and every class among the inhabitants of that area demonstrated a longing to be in our company and enter into discussion with us. Without exception these people showed us love and compassion. Some of them were indeed of noble nature. They did everything in their power to make us happy by their sincere love and often by their gifts. Some went so far as to ask us to give them the text of special prayers for the fulfillment of their wishes and the solution of their difficulties. During the fifty days of our imprisonment I was busy writing prayers, including verses that proclaimed the advent of the Báb and Bahá'u'lláh.

These fifty days enabled us to regain our energy, health, and strength. Every minute of those days we were far from the material world and very close to our Beloved because of the Tablets and prayers that we chanted. We were even ready to be martyred in His path. It would be better to be martyred here, we thought, than in the house of the Persian consul. In those days, because of the many cruelties we had suffered, our blood was thin and weak. After fifty days of rest and proper food, we felt that we had more and better blood to offer.

But all these were wishful thoughts, for the night arrived when the soldiers came to take us back to Egypt. These soldiers proved to be very kind indeed. They did not cause us difficulties, nor did they torture us on the way back. On the contrary, they allowed us to ride on camels, horses, and whatever was available. They also stopped at two or three stations to have coffee and tea and allow us to rest before continuing our journey.

When we approached a town, we were again put in chains, but the kindhearted soldiers apologized by saying, "We are under strict orders, and we have to surrender you to the authorities in chains." We were then taken to the first place to which we had been sent in our exile. The officers told us, "You are brought here for investigation."

But after six days, we were again sent to the former prison in the same chains and along with the same guards and officers. We reached our prison, and on the sixteenth day the soldiers took us to ironsmiths and carpenters in order to place permanent fetters on our feet and chains around our necks. This process proved to be more painful than anything which we had previously endured. We could not control ourselves and cried out in pain. The soldiers, blacksmiths, and carpenters wept at our plight. This was particularly true of the blacksmiths and carpenters, who cursed their professions for making them instruments for the torture of innocent people.

The last operation was to put our hands in stocks. The heavy fetters on our feet, the terrible chains on our necks and hands made every little movement a torment. We could not move our hands much, nor was it possible for us to lift the chains on our feet in order to make their weight less painful while walking.

The fashioning of the chains and the stocks began about two o'clock in the afternoon and was finished a little after sunset. Then they took us to a steamer and delivered us to a group of a hundred officers and soldiers.

We began to understand the evil instigations of the consul. He had so terribly frightened the Egyptian government that the boat carrying us refused to accept commercial goods lest the people should come to the ports, see our plight, and discuss the inhuman manner of our treatment. Whenever the boat drew near the shore and dropped anchor, we were immediately pushed into a storeroom the windows of which were firmly shut.

During our captivity, our clothes had never been changed. We had worn them for months and they became so torn and dirty that they were intolerable. Now that we were chained, we could not even take them off to wash them.

Gradually, God inspired the hearts of the guards and soldiers, and they took a liking to us. Out of pity they prepared us long, white garments. They had to tear the clothes off our bodies. Then, they washed us with hot water and clothed us with the new long robes. We felt so happy that we thought it was New Year's Day and we were wearing clothes for the festivities.

We discovered that those soldiers had been told that this humble servant could control spirits and influence invisible creatures. Therefore, they approached me and asked me to give them amulets to protect them against the operations of the spirits called "jinn," which they believed lived underground. I knew that the amulets which they were accustomed to contained the names of angels and numerological formulas. So I wrote some tablets for them in which I used the Greatest Name [24] and the anagrams for the names of Bahá'í friends. Sometimes I would add the names of the gifts which were brought to us, such as cheese, tobacco, bread, shirts, and tea. I write this particularly to show the reader that we were joyful and content in our imprisonment.

Ja'far Pá<u>sh</u>á, the governor-general of the Sudan, came on board our ship. He sent for me, and I was taken to his presence. I asked him, "What are the charges against us?"

"May God punish your consul," was his reply. "He has created such fear in the hearts of the government officials that all are afraid of you. He has accused you of changing your religion, your Book, and the Holy Laws of Islam. He says that you are terrorists and that you intend to assassinate the heads of government. But it is obvious that you are people of the path [25] and that you do not meddle in politics." He told us that he would see to it that we were made as comfortable as possible. However, we remained in that spot only three days.

On the third day, the guards were changed, and new ones came with camels for us to ride. But chained together as we were, our feet in one stock and our wrists joined by chains, how could we ride on camels? The guards were at a loss for what to do and how to carry us to our next destination. Eventually they brought some long pieces of strong, white cloth. They placed the hands and feet of each pair of us on the saddle, one person hanging on one side of the camel, and the other on the other side. Then they tied our hanging bodies to the camels with the white cloths. A more torturous way to travel cannot be imagined!

Five or six times during the short journey they made the camels kneel down, and we were untied and permitted to have a little rest. The guards apologized to us, saying that previously they had taken a group of thieves and murderers to the Sudan in chains, but that these others had to walk all the way through the desert. Ja'far Páshá had instructed them to allow us to ride, and they could not think of any other way. Although we were in great pain and torture, as we watched each other hanging from the camels, the sight was so ridiculous that we could not help laughing.

In five or six hours we reached the banks of the Nile River where we were again sent to a ship. We boarded and set off. The ship deposited us at a place that was under the control of a very kindhearted Arab shaykh. We explained our situation to him and asked him to treat us with more mercy. We still had a long stretch of desert to cover by camel. When the shaykh learned of our plight, he ordered the camel drivers to have wooden seats provided for us on the camels and to carry enough food for all. The shaykh was well experienced and knew how severe the desert journey would be. We had to travel twelve days over an ocean of sand.

In place of Egyptian guards, we were now entrusted to Arabs who were cruel hearted, devoid of manners, and very hot tempered. The moment we were in their hands they made it clear to us that they possessed the power of life or death. No matter what they did, no one was to complain or utter a word. The shaykh had supplied them with enough provisions for all, but these people only gave us enough for one person and consumed the rest themselves. Their treatment called to mind the hardships we had endured in the house of the consul in Egypt. Still we remained happy and could always find something to laugh at. We made jokes about our guards in Persian and would laugh heartily. When we finally reached the Sudan, we thanked God that we were alive.

OUR GUARDS brought us to the prison of the Sudan and the jailers immediately put us into a small, dark, and putrid cell. There were so many people crowded together that we could not even breathe, let alone move. The slightest gesture would arouse the anger of the jailers. We were surrounded by darkness, mosquitoes, fleas, lice, all manner of filth, and prisoners who were worse than scorpions. This proved to be the worst place we had been imprisoned. We were absolutely at a loss for which way to turn and what to expect.

Eventually I mustered my courage and begged the guard to take a message to the officer in charge. Fortunately he did this for me, and I was taken to the officer. Upon entering his room I said to him, "I am skilled in calligraphy and can write and arrange beautiful tablets. Would you kindly provide me with paper, ink, and pen?" He prepared everything for me, and I wrote a verse for him that said, "I surrender all my affairs to God." He was very pleased with the work and accepted it as a gift from me. After that he respected me. I told him that two of my companions were excellent calligraphers, another was a physician, and two were engravers. I also told him that we were prepared to do anything he might be pleased to order. So we were transferred to another room but still kept in chains. We rejoiced at the improvement in our condition.

Gradually we became known by the officers, guards, and prisoners. We transcribed many prayers for them, some of which would take us as much as two weeks to finish. Whatever gifts we received in return for our work, we immediately handed over to the jailer who had first taken our message to the officer. But he still kept us chained, two by two. No one can ever imagine the difficulties and hardships being chained in this position involved. To wash one's hands and face and attend to the other demands of nature was hell in itself.

After forty days they found that all the prisoners who were due to assemble there had arrived. A ship was made ready to take us to another prison in Khartoum.

Words fail to describe the foul language used by our fellow prisoners. Vile words and curses, epithets of blasphemy and damnation were freely, repeatedly, and shamelessly used by all. This group of bold, arrogant, and ferocious beasts took pride in exchanging stories of their thefts and escapes, their acts of murder and brutality toward others. They looked at us in disparagement and taunted us, saying, "Look, we have done all these courageous things. What have you done? Nothing. We are ashamed to be on the same boat with you."

There were some women prisoners on board, too. There was also a blind man who ceaselessly chanted the Qur'án. One day the women complained that someone had stolen their scissors. The guards searched everyone and everywhere. I could see that the blind man became pale and excited when the search began. Then the guards started beating the prisoners, one by one, in an effort to locate the scissors. So, to free the others from this misery, I told the soldiers that they should search the blind man. They found the missing scissors in his pantaloons.

Our trip was to have lasted six days, and enough provisions had been stored for this period. But because there was no favorable wind to fill the sails, we remained on board the ship for thirty-six days. Corn flour had been provided which we could bake, but with such malevolent companions, we were unable to approach the scanty provisions.

One day, while the boat was anchored, the guards told us that within two-hours' walk there was a village where we could find some food. Because we had gone several days with nothing but water, we had become very weak. Now, walking in chains for more than two hours was a great challenge to our determination. Nevertheless, we set out on foot. Constantly falling down and pulling ourselves to our feet, we finally reached the village, where we fainted and remained unconscious. Some people took pity on us and gave us sweet coffee to drink. They gave us a paste which looked like flour and water to eat. We thought that we had to cook it, but they told us it was already cooked. As we ate, I asked someone in Arabic what it was. He answered in a funny manner, and we all laughed so much that we almost forgot about our condition. Still, we had to return to our ship on foot.

We sailed slowly and reached another port, where we stayed about twelve days waiting for favorable winds to blow. Some of these days were comparatively happy and comfortable. We wrote amulets for the inhabitants of the village where we were staying, and they gave us provisions for the rest of the trip. Eventually we reached our final destination, the city of Khartoum.

ALL THE PRISONERS were afraid that they would be sent to the prison in Fashúdih, which was said to be the grave of prisoners. The weather there was supposed to be extremely unhealthy, and the prisoners were condemned to hard labor. We also learned of another prison close by called the "Dungeon of Fear." Since the ship to Fashúdih only traveled there every three or four months, prisoners were kept in this place until they could be transferred. It was indeed with sinking hearts that we heard about all these places.

Ja'far Páshá, the governor-general, arrived and sent for us. He assured us that he would do his utmost to keep us happy and comfortable. He then ordered the officers to take us to the nearby prison, change our heavy chains for light ones, exempt us from work, and cause us no trouble. He also recommended that we be separated from the rest of the prisoners. Before he sent us away, he remarked, "Love emanates from the heart. But a wise man must hide his love when he sees that others like him are cast into prison, and made to undergo grave difficulties, and have their property confiscated. One may love; but in case of danger, one should hide his feelings."

I made no reply but returned to my prison room. There I wrote a tablet for him. In large letters I wrote the following:

O you who accuse me of love!
If you understood my crime,
you would not blame me.

Around the edges of these words, I transcribed two recognized Muslim traditions. The first read: "Whosoever seeks Me, shall find Me. Whosoever finds Me, shall love

Me. Whoso loves Me, him shall I also love. Whoso is loved by Me, him shall I slay. Whoso is slain by Me, I Myself shall be his ransom."

Finally I wrote the second tradition: "How can one deny his love while two witnesses are testifying—one's tears and the paleness of one's face?" I sent this tablet to the governor-general through our guard.

When the guard returned, he related the following: "Ja'far Páshá says that the person who sent this tablet is a learned and accomplished man. He gives the correct answer to an argument and with a great deal of courtesy." The governor-general had also sent two gold coins to me.

THE DUNGEON in which we found ourselves consisted of a large cell which had only two doors. Each of the four hundred prisoners there had no more than the space of two hand spans in which to sit, sleep, and live. We had no proper clothes; the long shirts we had been given on the journey were so badly torn in several places that they did not even cover us. In this filthy cell, malodorous and full of obscenity, we struggled to hold on to life.

One day Ja'far Páshá summoned the jailer and asked him about our condition. The jailer gave him a true reply. "Because of the lack of space, intense heat, and filthy conditions, they are in grave danger." On hearing this, Ja'far Páshá ordered the jailer to make us a cottage of mats, timbers, and dry grass, where we were allowed to sleep at night. But the heat in that cottage also proved to be unbearable.

In order to keep the guards awake all night, they were

ordered to call out numbers in turn. If one failed to respond, he would be punished. We pitied our guard and told him to go to sleep—that we would guard in his place, answering the call of other guards by shouting, "One! Two! Three!" for him. We were happy to replace the guard, for then we could stand outside under the canopy of the sky and enjoy the fresh air. But we still remained deprived of every comfort of life. No pots or pans were given us—not even a cup or glass for drinking water.

Our daily ration was a handful of kernels of corn. We had to grind and knead our own flour and then make a fire and bake the loaves. We did not even have a copper coin with which to buy salt. But after a while we were able to earn some money, and we could afford to have our corn baked for us. The first time we had this done, we rejoiced with a real celebration. We were even more joyful when we finally obtained cups for drinking, rugs, and sleeping benches. We spent eight or nine months in the "Dungeon of Fear," and we were content and happy and thankful. From all sides, the doors of generosity were opened to us.

A Christian by the name of Búlus (Paul), who as the richest man in Sudan was the honorary consul of Persia, came to know of our condition. He was kind to us and sent us clothes, coffee, a lantern, and some mats. To express our thanks I wrote the name of Jesus Christ in Arabic calligraphy and arranged it in the shapc of a cross. In the margin I wrote that since Jesus had found His way to His Beloved through the cross, this was a sacred and exalted form. I also made another one of these tablets for the German consul, who was also a Christian but of a Protestant sect. The German consul, in return, sent us a samovar and the means for preparing tea.

Now we had enough provisions and could even invite

the other prisoners to tea. Gradually the people of Khartoum heard about us, and many of them from Muslim, Christian, and Jewish backgrounds came, individually and in groups, to see us. We even had visitors from among the army and civilian officials. Many of them came with different gifts. Whatever we received we shared with the guests and with our fellow prisoners.

Many strange events took place in that prison, some of which seem incredible. For example, there was a man named Joseph, who, because he committed thefts even in prison, had come to be known as "Rat." He was so shameless in his deeds and manners that I requested my friends not to associate with him. There was a woman, who had been caught in sin, who also lived in this prison. This same "Rat" took her as his wife. There was no privacy, but they slept together regardless of the presence of four hundred other prisoners.

Once we learned that "Rat" and his wife had been hungry for two days. As Bahá'ís we could not remain heedless of such a situation. I wrapped a gold coin in a piece of cigarette paper and offered it to him. When he saw the money, he became very courteous and even promised to reimburse us in the future. After that, he attached himself to me and I happily gave him a share of everything I had.

It then happened that some prisoners got together to devise a way to escape from the prison. They decided to cut the chains off each other's feet while they were grinding the corn. The noises were so mingled that none of the guards could detect the unusual sound of the file cutting through the fetters on the prisoners' feet. This took place at night, and eventually eight of them succeeded in ridding themselves of their chains. They rushed out suddenly, threw the guards to the floor, and ran away. The soldiers followed and caught four of them, but the remaining four threw themselves into the Nile, swam across the river, and disappeared.

The following day, the prison was a changed place. It was as if hell had opened its doors to us. The jailers and guards were changed, and new rules, regulations, and restrictions were instituted. Everyone was chained together. Harsh interrogations began, and those who were involved in the plot to escape were condemned to death by firing squad.

We were not even remotely involved in the plot. But all of a sudden the entire weight of this ill-fated venture fell upon our heads. Who had accused us? It was "Rat," who had approached the officers and told them that the Persians owned a file and had given it to the prisoners to effect their escape. We could not sleep the whole night, fearing that fresh attacks and new cruelties would be heaped upon us. Finally, I opened the Qur'án, and the first verse I saw, I read. It indicated that, on the morrow, the evildoers would be lined in a row in one chain. We took this as a sign that we ourselves would not be harmed. So we decided to try to be of service to others who were in trouble.

When the sun rose the next morning, we saw four gallows raised in front of our prison cell. All of the prisoners were taken out of the cell in chains, surrounded by guards; and we were among them. We were seated in a circle in front of the gallows. The commanding officer came forth with guards who had drawn swords in their hands. They marched up and down before the prisoners, ordering and shouting. Then there was silence, and the officer declared that the Persian prisoners had nothing to do with the escape. The soldiers removed our chains. We left the circle and immediately hastened inside because we could not bear the sight of the prisoners being hanged. For three days and nights thereafter, all the other people in the prison were chained together, and we served them with all our hearts and souls.

THE BENEVOLENT Ja'far Páshá wrote favorably about us to his government, telling them that the Persians were well educated and of good breeding and manners, that they had never done any harm to the people, and that, on the contrary, they had proved to be very useful citizens. He therefore asked that we not be transferred from "The Dungeon of Fear." For this reason we were not sent to Fashúdih as about one hundred other prisoners, including "Rat," were.

In Khartoum there was a blind man of extraordinary intelligence, by the name of Shaykh Amín, who had been appointed the Shaykhu'l-Islám of the city. I wrote him a letter which was quite a long dissertation on the history of the Cause. The concluding words were about ourselves imprisoned because of the cruel and unjust reports made by the Persian consul to the Egyptian government. This blind man saw that we had been treated with injustice. He took our letter to the governor, Ja'far Páshá, and requested him to see to our affairs. It was not long before the governor himself came to the prison and summoned us to his presence. He asked, "Which one of you wrote the letter to the Shaykhu'l-Islám?"

"We did," was our answer.

"I have heard that you are well educated and intelligent. But I asked you a question and you did not give me a proper answer."

I answered him, saying, "We are so overjoyed that such a high-ranking person should bestow such care and consideration on us that we do not know what we are saying. We know that in the presence of great ones such as yourself it is not proper to say very much. Moreover, we do not know your language, and therefore each of us may have a different idea of what you have said. And, finally, since we have all answered, one of us must be right, so we should not all be held responsible for a false answer."

He was very happy with my reply and ordered chairs to be brought so we could sit. When we were seated he said, "Ever since I first saw you, I have done my utmost to make life easier for you; and I will continue to do so." Then he asked the guards to remove our chains and transport us to a jail in Khartoum. Out of kindness, he urged the custodian of the jail not to be very severe with us. He told the custodian that we should be permitted to be free during the daytime and be allowed to go into the streets and markets. Instead of the ration of corn, we now had wheat bread, which was given to us with some meat every day. When we reached Khartoum, we were allowed to open our own businesses. Two of us started engraving. Ḥáji 'Alí became a physician and 'Alí Effendi, a teacher of English.

One of us, Ḥájí Abu'l-Qásim, kept to himself most of the time. He constantly recited prayers to himself. He was shrewd in business but also a bit miserly. When the rest of us went to Khartoum, he decided to remain in the prison. Since we were allowed to buy our food at the market, this friend would go to the prisoners, collect orders, and then visit the market. When he came back, he would sell them what they ordered, adding a good margin of profit for himself. Gradually he became rich, but he always satisfied himself with the corn given to the prisoners, selling his share of bread and meat to us.

Little by little, our prison cell became the town coffeehouse. Many people from different classes of society would come to us, and we entertained them with tea, coffee, sweetmeats, and even the water pipe. They asked me to make Persian rice for them. Because they brought me many gifts, I found it only fair to treat these guests with similar generosity.

Some of the most prominent people, and even some of the learned, believed that I had a strange mastery of witchcraft, capturing spirits, conquering the devil, and even ruling the sun. Once, while we were in the "Dungeon of Fear," a shaykh was brought who had a reputation for being able to control spirits. I asked him how skillful he was at this art. He replied, "I am able to write a verse on the fingernail of any person which will cause a jinn to visit him that very night."

"You are not a master," I said. "I can call for a jinn to come right now to attack you and beat you." And I started to summon an evil spirit. He became very fearful and excited and begged me to stop. So, I forgave him. I told him that the spirit would visit him, but that he would not be harmed.

Innumerable and incredible superstitions prevailed among the inhabitants of this part of the world. For example, if someone, particularly a woman, became ill, they firmly believed that the patient's heart had been stolen. Groups of men and women would surround the patient's bed and spend hours playing music, singing songs, and telling stories. This was supposed to encourage a jinn to come and prompt one of the people to speak and say something like, "Give so much money to such and such a man." They believed that when the money was paid, the stolen heart would be returned.

OUR BENEFACTOR, Ja'far Páshá, was replaced by Ismá'íl Páshá, who also proved to be very kind to us. He did his best to protect us from the onslaught of the ill-wishers. Although Ja'far Páshá had written to the government recommending that we be released from the prison, had given us permission to live in the town and freed us to earn our own living, it was during the rule of his successor that the affirmative answer reached the Sudan. The new páshá was very happy that during his regime we would be able to enjoy freedom from the prison and its hard labor, restrictions, and filthy atmosphere. He was so kind and gentle that he paid the first year's rent on my house.

Unfortunately, his rule did not last longer than six months. He had more enemies than friends, and he found himself faced with a committee of investigation. This proved exceedingly hard for him to bear. During this very difficult period in his life, we approached his house and asked if we could see him. As he knew that we were sincere, he gave us an audience. In the course of the conversation we mentioned that should the charges laid against him by his enemies prove to be true, there was one door always left open by God, and that was the portal of repentance. For God has promised in His Book to be compassionate and forgiving to anyone who approaches Him in remorse and repentance. However, if he had been wrongly charged by his enemies, he must remain happy and contented and surrender his will and his affairs into the hands of the All-Merciful.

In the end, the páshá's assistant became the governor, but he retained all the military affairs under his control. He continued to be very kind and considerate to us and appointed me as a teacher of Arabic grammar in the government schools. I taught only in the mornings, and I spent my afternoons copying the Qur'án and several collections of prayers.

THROUGH ALL THESE YEARS, we remained ignorant of what had happened to Bahá'u'lláh. We did not know of His exile to the Holy Land. We longed to know something about Him, but we had no way of reaching His presence. We sent letters to Adrianople in care of our Jewish, Christian, and Muslim friends, but we had no confirmation that they were ever received.

There was, however, a Christian friend by the name of Ilyás (Elijah), who was very kind and fair-minded in his judgment. For example, in our discussions with him we learned that he believed the Qur'án was superior to all the Books of God preceeding it. He knew of our deprivation and anxiety and promised to send our letters to Bahá'u'lláh in care of his friends, relatives, and business associates in Damascus, Beirut, and elsewhere.

How could we know that Bahá'u'lláh and His companions had been sent to 'Akká and had been living in very strict bondage? It was only afterwards that we learned that people such as Jináb-i-Nabíl had been trying for more than six months to have just a glimpse of Him.

It was during this period of our anxiety that Ḥájí Jásim-i-Baghdádí arrived, clad in the robes of a dervish. He had traveled all the way from the Holy Land to the Sudan. As promised by Bahá'u'lláh, he found us in the Sudan. No words can describe the depths of our joy and gratitude. It was as if the Sun of Truth had sent the penetrating rays of His love into the darkness of our prison life. Ḥájí Jásím's stay lasted for forty days, during every moment of which we discussed nothing and heard nothing except the stories of His exiles, the restrictions of life in 'Akká, and news of the beloved friends.

When the people of Sudan learned that a messenger had come to us from the country of our Beloved, they were astonished at this unexpected expression of love. The Muslims described it as an act of the promised Qá'im, and the Christians said that only Jesus would perform such a loving act. The fame of this divine gesture went far and wide, and many prominent citizens from all backgrounds—Turks, Egyptians, Arabs, Christians, and Muslims—invited Ḥájí Jásím to their own houses. In all these gatherings, we spoke openly about Bahá'u'lláh, His exiles, and His plight in the Prison of 'Akká. They all knew that Ḥájí Jásím had been specially sent to the Sudan to inquire about out situation.

While Ḥájí Jásím was still with us, our friend Ilyás Effendi brought us a Tablet of Bahá'u'lláh which had been sent in answer to our supplication. Our happiness on receiving this Tablet was immeasurable. We read the Tablet to Ilyás Effendi, who was deeply affected by its contents. He said that he believed in whatever we said, but that if only he could believe in the lesser prophets of the Bible, he would believe that the author of this Tablet was the true Father of Jesus Christ. He often said that he longed to become like one of the believers. Once I wrote to him that it is said that the Prophet Elijah (Ilyás) is living. "I believe with all my heart and soul that you are the living Elijah because you found my Beloved and brought me a message from Him."

Ḥájí Jásím returned to the Holy Land, but ever afterwards we were honored to receive at least five Tablets every year from the Blessed Beauty and regular news from the Holy Land and from His holy presence.

I feel obliged to mention Ḥájí Aḥmad of Mílán in Ádhirbáyján. It was because of the people who worked with him that we regularly received letters and news. All the friends knew of him and heard of his wonderful services to the Cause. His devotion, sacrifice, steadfastness, and detachment made him the unique servant of the Holy Threshold, and also to the Center of His Covenant. Who am I to praise him?

LET ME GO BACK to Ismá'íl Páshá, who proved a benevolent ruler of the country. He gradually made his way to higher and higher positions. The more he was promoted, the more he showed kindness toward us. In his earlier positions, he had never deigned to come to our place of residence, but once he had reached the highest position in the government he would often come to our house just to show his kindness toward us.

For a short time he was absent, and an official who worked in the office of publications and supervised the religious school began to spread false rumors about this servant. He claimed that I turned my pupils away from Islam and so lodged a complaint against me, which he had many people sign. He did everything in his power to destroy me. He had almost the entire population leagued with him, and I had to depend upon God alone. Because of his evil machinations, many did not dare to come near us.

The reader will remember Shaykh Amín, the blind

learned man of the Sudan. I had seen many such people, but none ever equal to him in learning and perceptive intelligence. Should a stranger pass by in the market-place or in the street, he would immediately declare that a stranger had passed by, because he had not heard his footsteps before. He could open any book to the page he desired. At this time, when my name was on the lips of all, and many believed the accusations against me, this noble person arose to defend the oppressed ones. He openly proclaimed that the Persians were of true faith, were noble in their deeds, and that such slanderous accusations were absolutely false.

The pá<u>sh</u>á returned home, and the moment he heard about the accusations he dismissed the official who had accused us and ordered an investigation of his affairs. It was soon discovered that this person had committed many unlawful things. He was then disgraced and lived all alone in his house. His own relatives would not go to see him, but they came to me and sought help for the management of the affairs of their household.

IT WAS IN THE seventh or eighth year of our imprisonment in the Sudan that Ḥájí 'Alíy-i-Yazdí, accompanied by his brothers, came to visit us, as instructed by Bahá'u'lláh. This bounty of God was indeed overwhelming. By this time we were financially well settled. What we needed was the breeze of the Merciful wafting over us from the rose garden of His love. This was granted to us by the coming of these friends, who brought fresh news from the Holy Land.

We suggested that one of them should stay in Khartoum to open and manage a commercial center. Ḥájí

'Alí accepted the proposal, and he himself became the head of this trading operation. The next year, I was in charge of this business, which in the course of time became very famous and a means by which many came to know about the Faith and its followers.

Once or twice a year someone would visit us from the Holy Land in the course of business. They would also bring the spiritual sustenance to keep us alive. We thanked God a thousand times that we had been favored with the knowledge of this Revelation.

At this time General Gordon became the governor of the Sudan. The person mentioned previously, who had falsely accused me in the past, now emerged from seclusion in his home to launch another attack against me, with more profane insults. He spared no efforts. Bribes were given in an attempt to poison the mind of the new governor against us. The first steps taken by this pernicious enemy seemed so injurious that we had cause to be alarmed. The governor, upon receiving these slanderous accounts, asked for reports from the English consul and others. All commended our small group and praised every one of us as noble citizens.

It was the custom at that time to set aside a special day when all the people would be invited to visit the new governor to welcome him and wish him a long and happy stay. When that day was announced, I prepared a mirror two-and-one-half meters in length and one-and-one-half meters in width. I had the mirror inscribed with mercury in large English letters: "Long Live General Gordon." I sent him this mirror in care of the British Consulate. It was so warmly received that they ordered another one to be made for General Gordon's sister in England, and they sent a hundred pounds for the gifts we had offered.

Because Bahá'u'lláh had, both verbally and in some Tablets, promised that I would meet Him again, even during the most trying moments of my captivity and imprisonment, in the innermost part of my heart I felt certain that the day would dawn when I could make my way once more to His presence. When the second mirror was offered to General Gordon, he very kindly remarked, "No amount of money could equal the excellence of your gift; therefore, you must tell me what I can do for you."

It was a most opportune moment and I said to him, "I want nothing except to free myself from this situation."

"Write a petition and explain that you were imprisoned without any inquiry or investigation," he replied. I prepared a petition saying that we all abhored what had been attributed to us, that kings and rulers have no sovereignty over the hearts and consciences of the people, and that no power except that of the Almighty could ever govern or control the hearts of men. Therefore, we requested to be set free and allowed to return to our homes. We concluded by stating that we would continue to pray for his just government. One of the other Bahá'ís wrote a similar petition.

This letter was dispatched to the general, and soon a cable was handed to us stating that we were free to return home, but we were not allowed to go to Egypt. The day of departure was indeed a great spectacle. All of the notables—Christians and Muslims—came to bid farewell and see us safely on board the ship bound for freedom.

After our departure, we learned that the consul general of Iran, Mírzá Ḥusayn Khán, who had committed so many iniquities and had been the cause of our imprisonment, eventually became the subject of the hatred of his own compatriots. The incessant plots he contrived against others for the purpose of depriving them of their possessions and money caused many oppressed individuals to lodge complaints against him to the Persian court. Officers investigated and soon his plans, plunders, and persecutions became known. First he was stripped of all the wealth he had so dishonestly gathered from Persian subjects. Then he was put in chains and dispatched to Persia. So he was punished for his evil deeds.

My boat was bound for Jiddih, the well-known Arabian port where thousands of pilgrims gather to approach Mecca and Medina. Wherever the boat docked, chiefs of the Arab tribes showed us much kindness and hospitality. When we landed in Jiddih, I turned toward Mecca and said, "Yes, my Lord, I am here."

In Mecca a great surprise awaited me. Upon my arrival I had the immense joy and honor of meeting two Bahá'ís, Salmán, "the messenger of the Merciful," and Ḥájí Muḥammad-i-Yazdí.

After spending two months in quarantine, we left Mecca. Crossing the tempestuous sea, we saw at every moment the wings of death spread over us. After losing all hope of arriving anywhere, we finally reached Beirut. In this city we had the honor of meeting Muḥammad Muṣṭafá Baghdádí. He was one of the most distinguished followers of the Faith. From childhood he had faced the hardest tests and emerged stronger and with even more faith and certitude. He was staunch and steadfast, his heart filled with the intense heat of love and faithfulness. I have never met another person who could so perfectly offer the water of life to the friends, and at the same time the fire of God's wrath to the Covenant-breakers. His sons, Ḥusayn, 'Alí, and Ḍíá, carried the essence of their father. They all stood as members of one body to serve the Cause of God and the people of Bahá. Even the children were adorned with the robe of servitude. It seems that their mother had fed them with the milk of eternal life and had brought them up in the bosom of love and compassion. Truly, the father of this noble family was a Bahá'í in name, deeds, life, and in every atom of his existence. While in the presence of this unique and wondrous family, I could inhale the sweet perfume of servitude to 'Abdu'l-Bahá.

It was in their house that I wrote a supplication to Bahá'u'lláh in the Holy Land. At the top of my letter I wrote a verse of the Qur'án which reads: "Praised be the Lord Who has fulfilled His promise and granted us the earth as our inheritance and to live in Paradise as we wish." But in the letter I changed "as we wish" to "as Thou desirest." When my letter reached His merciful hands, He immediately said, "We have invited him long ago. He is permited to come."

AFTER THREE DAYS we reached 'Akká, the city which is praised and extolled in the Holy Books of the past. There were three persons in the Pilgrim House who could be called the chosen ones of God and the essences of existence: Mírzá Muḥammad Ḥasan, the caretaker of the Pilgrim House and a true servant to all the visitors; Ḥusayn Áqá, who like a light of faithfulness constantly hovered near Bahá'u'lláh awaiting His every wish; and Mírzá Áqá Ján, who was in the presence of the Ancient Beauty. The first two were never deceived by the rank and position given them, but the third one could not stand firm against the suggestions of self. Eventually, his nearness was changed into everlasting loss.

The first two had sacrificed themselves utterly to their Beloved and to the services granted them to perform. We never heard a word from them which could denote personal ambition. The Persian poet says:

For their Beloved, the lovers die.
They have no words to make reply.

Because of my long imprisonment, my eyes had become weak. For a considerable time it had been difficult for me to read and write. Once 'Abdu'l-Bahá entered our room at the Pilgrim House and asked me about the condition of my eyes and ears. When I explained, He recommended that I not shave my head.[26] He explained that it was against the explicit text of the Kitáb-i-Aqdas. He advised me to let my hair grow and to begin to write, even if only ten words a day. "As you regain your eyesight, you should increase the amount of writing," was His loving recommendation to me. Now I am more than eighty years of age, but the weaknesses of my eyes and ears have never reached so low a condition as they were thirty-five years ago in the Sudan.

At night we were called upon to attend the presence of Bahá'u'lláh. As a Muslim I had learned that there are many categories of angels. Some constantly stand in prayer, while others sit, mentioning His names and attributes, and still others remain prostrated in front of Him. But the highest rank of angels are those who remain bewildered and awestruck by the beauty and splendor of the Beloved.

I found true examples of the last group of angels in the Bahá'í community of 'Akká. They numbered more than a hundred, each one united to the other like members of one body. They were proud of each other, and the bond which joined them together in perfect unity was nothing but their selfless love for the Glory of God. Most of them were busy during the day in their shops; but three hours before sunset, they gathered near the house of Bahá'u'lláh. Some would seat themselves on the steps, while others would walk slowly and talk of nothing but His words and His desires.

Sometimes they could behold Him walking on the balcony of His house. Their joy would know no bounds if He would beckon to them to hasten to His room. They were so united that they would sacrifice everything for each other. Whenever a group of them was granted permission to go to Him, all the others shared their spiritual ecstasy. It seemed that their exultation affected the whole surroundings. One could feel the effect of their rapturous state even in the atmosphere. And they had every right to reach such a state of intoxication because they were allowed to enter the Paradise of Reunion. It was extremely interesting to see them when they returned. For a long period of time they would remain quiet. When they were themselves again, they would report to the others the sweet words they had heard. Invariably they confessed that their words were not the exact utterances of Him in Whose presence they had stood, totally enraptured.

As far as I remember, there was no one who claimed to utter one complete sentence in His presence. Of course, there were some arrogant souls who reached the Land of Promise and sought His audience for the sake of argument, debate, or dispute. Even such people were graciously permitted to go to Him. Very often it happened, however, that the moment they heard His voice saying, "Please come in," they would enter His room, prostrate themselves, and then remain seated, unable to utter a word. Thus they were transformed and went home sincere and full of love and faith. There were, of course, some exceptional cases. Some of the nonbelievers experienced the same feeling of overwhelming spiritual power but on going home declared, "We were bewitched."

Bahá'u'lláh's imprisonment in the walled city of 'Akká for nine years became a source of deep sorrow to the beloved Master, 'Abdu'l-Bahá. Therefore, He purchased land between two rivers and planted some flowers and trees there. Later this place became known as the Garden of Riḍván (Paradise).[27] The work involved in constructing this garden took six or seven years to complete. But Bahá'u'lláh would not accept the proposal of even visiting the place. Outwardly He was a prisoner and refused to go without the permission of the state. 'Abdu'l-Bahá asked the mufti of 'Akká to speak to Bahá'u'lláh. He instructed him to enter His room and not to leave unless and until He agreed to visit the garden. The officials of the government did not have the slightest objection to His going there.

The mufti obtained permission to enter Bahá'u'lláh's room. He approached, prostrated himself, and held the hem of the garment of the Blessed Beauty. Bahá'u'lláh tried to pull away the hem, but the mufti said, "I will not let it go until you grant my wish."

Bahá'u'lláh smiled and asked, "What do you want?"

The mufti said, "Nothing but this: That the garden become the Garden of Riḍván through the honor of your presence." When He gave His consent, the mufti hastened out to give the good news to 'Abdu'l-Bahá and the government officials.

THREE MONTHS PASSED and I was still a pilgrim. During this time, 'Abdu'l-Bahá arranged to rent the Mansion of Mazra'ih, where Bahá'u'lláh lived for two years. I remember that once the Riḍván Feast was celebrated in the house of Jináb-i-Kalím,[28] where I was living. A new pá<u>sh</u>á had arrived in 'Akká as the head of the Custom House. On that day he was sitting in a coffeehouse with many of his officers and other dignitaries of the town. Bahá'u'lláh was on His way to His brother's house. As He passed the coffeehouse, the pá<u>sh</u>á and all his retinue stood up and bowed before Him. As He passed by, He bestowed His loving benediction upon them. Then the pá<u>sh</u>á, bewildered, approached his friends and asked, "Is this the Holy Spirit or the King of Kings? Who is He?"

"He is the father of 'Abbás Effendi," [29] was the unanimous reply.

I HAD SUCH wonderful companions that I never wished to be separated from them. They were Jináb-i-Nabíl, the historian; Mírzá Muḥammad Ḥasan, the custodian of the Pilgrim House; and Darví<u>sh</u> Sidq-'Alí, one of the companions of Bahá'u'lláh in His exiles and imprisonment. We gathered together in the neighborhood of our Beloved and spent the evenings in the mention of God. Because of our spiritual meetings, the night became more illumined for us than the day.

Darvísh Sidq-'Alí, before embracing the Faith, had been addicted to opium. Now that he had stopped using it, breathing became very difficult for him. Once, for an entire night he struggled to breathe. The doctors recommended that he return to opium, so he asked permission of Bahá'u'lláh to use a little. Instead, he was given a gold coin with which to purchase medicine.

Fearing death, he came to us and said that it was contrary to detachment and absolute dependence on God to have such an amount of money in his purse. He could not reconcile himself to what he felt was a departure from spiritual law. But as Bahá'u'lláh had told him that He liked people to have some capital, he thought that the best investment for his money would be to purchase sugar and tea and offer them to the Holy Household. His offering was graciously accepted because his reasons were logical and acceptable.

THE DAY CAME when I was to return home—but how could I leave the Paradise of Reunion? Twice I sent letters, and twice permission was granted me to stay another two weeks. When the third time came and I was asked to go, I went to 'Abdu'l-Bahá and explained how unbearable it was for me to leave the presence of Bahá'u'lláh. I was summoned to go to Bahá'u'lláh's room. He smiled and told me, "You can stay fifteen days more, but on the condition that someone will guarantee your departure at that time. We want you to return home very happy, but do not forget the condition: someone must guarantee that you will leave!"

To this I promptly replied, "The Master!" [30]

He smiled and agreed that I could stay fifteen days more. When I reached the Pilgrim House, I actually danced to show the uncontrollable joy that had overwhelmed me.

During my last fifteen days, I was very often in the presence of 'Abdu'l-Bahá. I have no words to explain the enchantment of my soul nor can I repeat the sweet utterances I heard. I can never be grateful enough for all the divine bounties which were abundantly showered upon me. I was sent to the Sudan as a humble prisoner and captive, and now I had emerged from the darkness of imprisonment to behold the wondrous countenance of Bahá'u'lláh and 'Abdu'l-Bahá. Then, I was poor and destitute; now, I had gold coins and material possessions. Spiritually and materially I was now in a perfect condition. How could I ever express my gratitude?

As I was pondering such thoughts in 'Akká, the beloved Master asked me, "Would you be happy if you lost all that you now possess?"

I replied, "I would be in the same position as when I left Persia years ago. I did not have a penny then—and now I will not mind if I am penniless when I return home. I do not care for anything, so long as I can keep my faith and love. You made me rich; when I offered my possessions to you, you accepted them and then returned them to me." At that time I could not understand what the Master intended by this conversation.

FINALLY the day came when I had to leave 'Akká for Iran. Many Tablets were entrusted to me, but 'Abdu'l-Bahá's instructions were very explicit:

"When you reach the soil of Iran, you must give all the Tablets to a trusted friend and ask him to forward them to wherever you choose as your future address."

I went to Iran by way of Mosul and Baghdád. In Mosul I had the great joy of visiting Jináb-i-Zayn and all the friends who had been captured in Baghdád and sent as prisoners to this northern district of Iraq. I lent the Tablets to Jináb-i-Zayn, who transcribed them. During my entire trip through various countries on my way to Iran, I was very courteously and respectfully received by the government officials, because they knew that I was an obedient servant of that illustrious person known as 'Abbás Effendi. Because of their loving attachment to the Master, the officials made every stage of my travel across their countries very comfortable and pleasant.

I also met my uncle, Jináb-i-Vakíl. As one of the captives, it was necessary for him to earn a living in order to provide for his family. At his advanced age he found no other way but to learn shoemaking. Though in a state of near poverty, he took me to his home. The love and hospitality that family showed put me to shame, especially when I could only express my gratitude in words—and promises of prayers on their behalf and on behalf of the deceased members of their family. These people lived in such unity, love, and peace that they mirrored forth the same light as one beheld in the Bahá'í community of 'Akká.

They vied with each other in serving the Cause and had no ultimate aim in life except to have a glance of His countenance. Though poor, they had established a fund to which the adults and children would contribute any extra amount from their daily income. In time of need the friends were allowed to borrow, but with the stipulation that they would pay back the loan with interest.

ON THE BORDER between Iraq and Iran I met someone from 'Akká. When he learned that I had spent some time there, he introduced me to the Kurds, and they enveloped me with love and hospitality. Some venerable men of that district related to me stories of the sojourn of the Ancient Beauty in the mountainous districts of their country and of the spiritual impact He had on all the people. They were so enthralled with one of the Tablets 'Abdu'l-Bahá had written at the age of fourteen, in which He had expounded on divine love, that within a few days they made at least ten copies of that long commentary.

There was a Persian residing there named Áqá Ján-i-Narághí. I learned that he had been a great opponent of the Cause and an enemy of the friends, for whom he had caused afflictions and persecutions. This man became a very firm believer during my stay amongst the Kurds, and he then arose to serve the Cause in order to compensate for his past errors. It happened that, on one of his trips, he and his companions were attacked by outlaws and robbed of their possessions. They found themselves penniless and with no means of livelihood. At that moment of distress and agony, he looked up to the heavens and said, "O God, is this the way to treat Áqá Ján?"

After saying this, he continued walking home. Some time later he received a Tablet from Bahá'u'lláh. In it He stated, "We heard your whisperings. You are right! God will be with you and will confirm you." From then on new doors were opened to him and to the other friends. They had great success in their services to the

Cause which they had recently and very courageously embraced.

Áqá Ján and I spent many hours, together with other Bahá'ís, trying to teach the Faith to the Kurds. It was difficult, but four or five people became believers, and we held some meetings for prayers and discussion. Though we did not allow people to know about our meetings and everything was conducted in a very quiet manner, one night we heard a knocking at the door. When we opened it, a man entered and told us that he was thirsty to know about the Faith. He was in tears and said, "You are known as the followers of a new religion. I have observed you and have found you to be people of purity, chastity, and piety. I nevertheless received reports of evil things about you. But when I observed those who spread these reports, I found them busy pursuing the material things of life. Sometimes I came across these people gambling or backbiting. In your conversation I heard nothing but the mention of God. Therefore, I believe that you are worshipers of God." After some discussion this man embraced the Cause.

Another person came and asked for the Kitáb-i-Íqán. He returned the next day and said, "When I went to my room and started reading the book, I stopped and decided that I would lock the door from within. I began to imagine all sorts of things: someone may have seen me lock the door and might guess I was reading a Bábí book. So I put out the light and retired early, in order to get up before dawn to read the book. Again an army of idle thoughts came to me: surely my neighbors will think that the reason for my going to bed in the early hours of the evening was to get up before dawn for no other purpose than to read Bábí books!

"I was beginning to feel at a loss for what to do and

to wonder how I should ever have the courage to read this book. A verse from the Qu'rán came to my mind. It says that assurance is granted to hearts only through the mention of God. I begged God, the Almighty, to strengthen my heart. As I was praying, something suddenly dawned upon me and I said to myself, 'You are frightened to death at the thought of merely reading this book. Ponder then the strength of heart which belonged to the One Who first wrote it. This same courage has been imparted to many others who willingly hastened into the arena of martyrdom.' "

These thoughts brought our friend to absolute faith. Though he was involved in extensive commercial enterprises, he spared no effort or time to copy Tablets and he was able to teach many others. The Persian poet says:

Make no search for water. But find thirst,
And water from the very ground will burst.

SINCE I HAD REACHED the soil of Persia, following the instructions of the Master I found a reliable friend by the name of Asadu'lláh, and I entrusted him with all the holy Tablets. I asked him to dispatch them to Tabríz. As for my matcrial possessions, I consulted with the friends on how best to invest my money so that the profit would enable me to travel and teach the Faith. The friends advised me to entrust my capital to the care of a respectable Bahá'í of Tabríz by the name of Ḥájí Aḥmad-i-Mílání. It never occurred to me to leave these material riches with those spiritual ones I had entrusted to Asadu'lláh. Neither I nor my advisors realized the reason for 'Abdu'l-Bahá's instructions. As the proverb says, "When the end has come, the best physicians are but fools."

One early morning we set off with a caravan heading for Tabríz. We had scarcely been on the way for more than half an hour when a group of thirty well-armed outlaws issued forth from the hills and spread themselves amongst the travelers. Everything we possessed was stolen—even our clothes were taken from us. We begged them to give us back enough clothing to cover ourselves, but they refused.

I had only one hope. As we had run away, I was able to throw a small pouch containing nineteen gold coins into a pit. After the outlaws abandoned us to our fate and the caravan drivers had scattered to rescue their mules, which had run away in different directions, I returned to the place where I had thrown the pouch and retrieved it. Then I made my way back to the house of friends where I had slept the night before. They brought me clothes to cover my nakedness.

Complaints were sent to the governor, but to no avail. I wrote a letter to the Holy Land and said in lighthearted fashion, "I obeyed, and entrusted all the Tablets and Holy Writings to a friend upon arrival in Iran; but what would have happened if the same instructions had been given for the care and protection of the property of this servant?"

Many people came to our help, but none ever succeeded in locating the highway robbers nor in retrieving our possessions. The last one who came to help us was Mírzá 'Abdu'lláh Khán, the maternal grandfather of Jináb-i-Varqá. It was a great honor to be with this friend and to be aware of his spiritual excellence. As the days passed, I thanked God every moment that the loss of those ephemeral possessions gave me a chance to spend a few days with him.

I spent four months in that region, making every effort to recover my possessions. But there was no hope. During this time I continued to teach, and several people became Bahá'ís—sufis, merchants, and shopkeepers. These victories were only the result of being robbed and wronged, and of my suffering and poverty.

AFTERWARDS, I traveled to Ṭihrán for a visit and also to earn a living and to teach the Faith. One Sunday I went to the service of a Protestant mission in the city. While there, I found an opportunity to talk about the Prophets of the past. The minister in charge was delighted and kept me after the service ended. We discussed different matters, and he found me to be sympathetic to the Protestant faith and so was kind to me.

But he was puzzled by my friendliness. He asked me who I knew among the noblemen of the city. I said that I had come to Ṭihrán only recently and that I was involved in cleansing my soul and therefore had met no one. This caused him to be even more curious about me. He appointed some people to spy on me and so discovered that I was a Bahá'í.

When I went to visit him again, he would not see me. "We receive one hundred thousand túmáns a year from the United States to teach the Faith of Christ," he said. "But you are a Bahá'í and have come here to infiltrate our group and hunt for converts."

"I have not come here to hunt for converts from your congregation," I replied, "but to find if you profess this faith for the sake of money or for the sake of God. Now I see that you love only money and power."

After this encounter, I did not know what to do. I seemed to be a lost soul. I wanted to earn some money and to serve the Cause of God, but it seemed impossible. At my age, if I entered a profession, I would have no skills or experience, and my work would allow me no time to teach. Then I realized that if I became a scribe, I could satisfy my needs and study the Sacred Writings as well. So I began to copy some of the Writings for a living. But I was entrapped in a spiritual dilemma.

I listened to the promptings of my own self, and it told me that in the Sudan we used to receive a Tablet at least every month or two. Then, Ḥájí 'Alí and Ḥájí Jásím were sent to convey messages of His love. Now, after all the sufferings that we had endured, ever since we had arrived in Iran there had been no message and no Tablet. Such vain imaginings caused me so much distress that I was nearly destroyed. I was immersed in a sea of despair. But soon I realized that my agony was due to nothing other than my own ignorance.

I continued to transcribe the Sacred Writings. One day, as I was copying the Hidden Words of Bahá'u'lláh, I came across the following verse:

> *O SON OF MAN!*
> *Humble thyself before Me, that I may graciously visit thee. Arise for the triumph of My cause, that while yet on earth thou mayest obtain the victory.*[31]

Suddenly all the past events of my life flashed before me. I examined them one by one, and as I found nothing except my lowliness, and the exaltedness of the bounties of God everywhere and in every instant of my life, I addressed myself saying, "Act not like the beggars who expect wages for every insignificant deed."

Fortunately, I was able to triumph over my despair and emerge with a new sense of happiness and responsibility. From then on I have refused to allow myself to feel sad and gloomy, even if all the friends should ignore me. This has never actually happened, but when the slightest suggestion of self would begin to overtake me, I would reproach my own self and say, "It is your own mistake!"

Because of this inner struggle, I was gradually able to reach a world of tranquillity and immeasurable spiritual exaltation. I was revived, and with a new spirit I hastened to the friends. Many a night we gathered together. The friends were few in number, and we were never apart. These few believers were poor, and everyone earned a meager living with great difficulty. One of them was Bábá-Ján, gatekeeper of the house of the Amínu'd-Dawlih. His lunch was provided for him by his master. He would bring this home, and, adding to it a small amount of cheese and yogurt, he would invite the friends to partake of this banquet. It would feed seven. At night he would provide us with ábgúsht (stew).

The only ones who were well off among the friends in Ṭihrán were Áqá Muḥammad Karím 'Aṭṭár and his brother, Ḥájí Muḥammad Raḥím. These two believers and their sisters were all devoted to the Cause of God. Whenever the friends desired to have a sumptuous meal, they would send them a message, and the family would comply with their wishes and send Persian rice and roast meat. One night the brothers themselves attended such a banquet, and the delicious food was followed by fresh fruit. We had a wonderful meeting together.

THE TIME CAME when I decided to travel to towns and villages in Iran for the purpose of teaching the Cause. In order to be successful during such arduous trips, I adopted the most simple mode of life. I traveled with the caravans. My food consisted of ábgúsht and milk, whenever I could get that. Words fail to explain how all my affairs were arranged, but He hastened to me by miles whenever I drew myself near to Him even as much as one step! Should the whole world ponder this miracle, it would prove impossible to understand or appreciate such mysterious divine bounties. How can we then fittingly express our gratitude? His bounties are endless and our words of praise totally inadequate.

In the course of my Bahá'í tours and teaching sessions, I could feel His invisible and transforming force, which possessed all hearts. Transformation and confirmation are powers which belong to God alone. It is only through His grace and bounty that we weak children are enabled to crawl on the path of servitude. Yet He appreciates our feeble efforts and crowns them with the laurels of His pleasure and acceptance.

For about thirty years I traveled throughout Iran. Should I try to describe all the fallacious arguments and protestations of the people and their bitter disapproval, the love and assistance of the friends, the answers which were given only through divine confirmation and inspiration, this little epistle would become a voluminous book.

IN KHURÁSÁN, the Shujá'u'd-Dawlih had met Fáḍl-i-Qá'iní (Nabíl-i-Akbar) and other illustrious Bahá'ís. But unfortunately some enemy of the Cause, under the pretense of being knowledgeable about the Faith, had met him and given him many wrong ideas against the Faith. Because of this, I very much desired to meet him so that I might dispel such false conceptions from the mind of this very powerful and influential governor.

One by one his servants came to see me. I asked them to arrange a meeting between their master and me, and lest he would be disturbed, I emphasized that such a meeting should be held secretly.

A meeting was therefore arranged. When I was admitted to his home, I said that I was a traveler. He immediately asked me if I had been to 'Akká and if I had met Bahá'u'lláh. My answer was affirmative.

"What is His claim?" he asked.

"He claims to be the Promise of all the Prophets of God," I replied. Then I recited many of the verses revealed by His exalted Pen. In conclusion I said that I did not consider myself to be one of His true followers, but endeavored to explain everything about them based on my own understanding and judgment.

He did not like my statement and he said, "If you were not one of His followers, you could not speak so fluently about Him and would not have memorized so many passages from His Writings. I know you are one of them; therefore, unveil yourself and speak to me openly."

When I confessed to him that I was one of the servants of the Cause, he showed me much kindness and commanded me to be in his presence every morning. He permitted me to withdraw only after the midday meal. During those days I explained every detail of the Faith to him—its history, principles, and precepts—and he embraced the Faith of God. Thereafter, people came to our meetings in large numbers.

Because of such victories, I wrote to Bahá'u'lláh and explained that I had spoken of the Faith openly. Soon I received a Tablet which was written in a joking style, yet was most alarming. Bahá'u'lláh stated that since I had confessed to Him that I had violated the principle of wisdom and had spoken openly about the Cause, I had made myself the object of sanction and must receive my punishment. But at the end of the Tablet He made me hopeful and happy by saying that God is always forgiving and compassionate. This Tablet warned me that certain unpleasant things were going to happen to me.

One of the friends told me that the governor had an extraordinary secretary. Should there be one hundred persons of outstanding intellectual faculties, he would surpass them all. But unfortunately he was an atheist and a drunkard. My friend urged that I see this extraordinary person. It was therefore arranged that I should meet him.

We began talking at about sunset, and we continued throughout the entire night. During the conversation, I did my best to open up a discussion on the Faith, but he stubbornly turned the conversation toward some other subject each time it began to veer in the direction of religion. He was indeed a master of the art of conversation. I was utterly absorbed by the facility with which he directed the flow of our discussion in whatever way he chose. The more he rebuffed my efforts to introduce the subject of religion, the more I liked him and the more I longed to teach him the Faith of Bahá'u'lláh.

In the morning I finally asked him, "Have you studied any of His Writings?"

"No!" was his immediate reply.

"Why not?" I asked. "You have such a large library and yet you have not read any of His books."

"I desire to live by my own free will," he answered.

I mustered my courage and, pointing to his books, said, "I believe this is sheer prejudice and nothing else. You do not believe in the contents of all these books, and yet you have them and read them. Were it not for this prejudice against the Manifestation of God and His works, you would not refrain from knowing something about our literature."

He said, "You have overpowered me. After our long wrestling match, now you have me flat on the floor. You are right. Send me a book and I will read it."

The Kitáb-i-Íqán was given to him. I saw him the next evening, and he told me that he had read the book at least ten times and was overcome with uncontrollable feelings for the revealed words and the One who had written such powerful utterances and mighty arguments. He wanted to copy it, but one of the friends gave him his book.

When he embraced the Faith, he broke all his barrels of wine and stopped using opium and other drugs. He became such a staunch supporter of the Cause that nothing could dampen his enthusiasm. He taught the Faith to his family and to many others; he met and openly challenged all the outstanding clerics of the province. No matter how we discouraged him, we could not prevent him from this open teaching.

The 'ulamá grew desperate. Mullá Káẓim, who was the religious leader of the town, went to the Shujá'u'd-Dawlih and asked him to banish or imprison me. But the governor said, "Come and debate with him. If he cannot stand your challenges, I will agree to any punishment—even his execution. If I send him away now, the people will believe that I have punished someone who was innocent. I never want to be accused of such a grave error."

The governor arranged for a meeting in his own presence. Many of the outstanding 'ulamá were there, and government officials as well as other observers stood by watching the proceedings. I began the discussion by asking the following question:

"Let us suppose that a Jew who, believing in the Old Testament, states that in more than fifty instances in that Book, God has mentioned that the Judaic dispensation would remain unchanged for eternity. Based on this, he does not believe in Jesus. There is also a Christian who says that it is explicitly stated in the Gospels that heaven and earth may pass away, but not a single word of this Book will ever be changed. This person denies anyone after Jesus. How does God judge such persons, and on what basis would they deserve the wrath of God and His punishment?"

"There are no such references," the 'ulamá replied. The book was brought and references were shown, after which they said, "Their books were altered by their followers."

I replied, "This is not possible. People who believe in a Holy Book will never change a single word of it. No thinking person could ever accept such an argument. Even if kings and divines join their forces to alter a word, it would prove absolutely impossible. This is because it is the Book of God and does not exist in only one town or one country. There are copies everywhere. So, even if a very powerful ruler changed some words in the books available in his own country, what about the copies of the same book in other countries and other continents of the world? Moreover, in all the revealed scriptures there is a promise given by God: 'We reveal the Book and we protect it.' In many instances in the Qu'rán, the Prophet Muḥammad, referring to the Jews and Christians, testifies that He approves and accepts the Books held in their hands."

The 'ulamá could not answer these proofs. They said, "Why do you speak only of pre-Islamic times and the Holy Books of the past?" So proofs from the Holy Qu'rán were also given.

The governor said, "His proofs are sound and you cannot deny them."

Mullá Káẓim became angry and left the room, saying,

"The governor supports the Bábís." He was brought back. When seated, he said, "What about the miracles?"

"In the Qu'rán," I started, "the Prophet Muḥammad has declared that the revealed words of God are His miracles."

"What about the moon which was split into two parts by just a movement of Muḥammad's finger?"

"Bahá'u'lláh declares that when He was in Adrianople, stars fell to the earth."

The governor interrupted by saying, "That is true. We were at the head of a very large army crossing the plains of Khurásán. During the night, suddenly, before our eyes stars began to pour down upon the earth. This spectacle continued for two hours. There were so many stars that the darkness of the night was changed to daylight."

"If the stars fell," Mullá Káẓim replied in a mocking tone, "what are these stars that we see in the sky?"

I replied politely, "If the moon was split, what is this round object that *we* see in the sky?" Everyone burst into laughter, and the governor prevented me from going on and asked me not to say anything more.

"We have gathered here to make things clear," he said. "But I see that the matter has only become more confusing. I fear that the faith of some good Muslims here may be shaken."

"Yes," Mullá Káẓim insisted. "These people are masters at deceiving others and causing doubts in people's faith. They have memorized ten weak verses of the Qu'rán and twenty doubtful traditions, and they are determined to mislead the whole population."

I replied, "Although I am forbidden to speak, I hope you will excuse me. I must say this one thing. Why don't you recite the strong verses and the authentic traditions and stop the people from being deceived?" Everyone laughed again.

This discussion continued for more than seven hours, after which the 'ulamá arose to go home. But I could see that evil plots were already stirring in their minds against the Bahá'ís. I weighed the situation in my mind: if I stay here, the sleeping giant of malevolence will be awakened; and if I go, the people will think me a coward. What should I do? The governor was one of the strongest and most determined rulers of the provinces of Persia; because of the flame of his wrath, no one would dare agitate the people. Therefore, I stayed and readied myself for the worst that might occur. I was quite certain that whatever took place would bring only exaltation and prestige to the Cause and aid its propagation throughout those regions.

THE NEXT DAY, when the sun rose, people rushed to my house like locusts from every direction, all armed with sticks and clubs. I put on my clothes and decided to go forth and meet the attackers. I thought that in this way the Holy Scriptures which I had in my home would be spared. When I stepped out, I found myself attacked by no less than two hundred wolves. As they dragged me to the theological school, they spared no opportunity to beat me and utter curses and words of profanity against the Faith.

Mullá Káẓim was standing in the school, surrounded by the angry mob. I asked for a glass of water. I knew that, since they were S͟hí'ihs, they could not deny my request for water,[32] and I could take the opportunity to gain some respite from their tortures. So water was brought. But the mullá shouted, "Shut his mouth!" They closed my mouth. Then the mullá approached and struck me on the head with his long stick.

"This is not enough," he told the mob. "You must stone him." I was forced out of the town and only God knows what befell me on the way to the outskirts of the city. They tortured me with sticks, clubs, stones, and fire. They finally imprisoned me in a small room situated far from the city walls.

After an hour, they returned and said, "The mullá has decreed that you should give us your books, after which you will be free to go wherever you choose. If you do not obey, he has told us to tear you to pieces." After a while the mullá himself came to my cell. He stood before the mob and ordered me to go wherever I desired. He would prevent the people from attacking me further, provided they could see me disappear over the horizon. The mullá and his followers stood and watched.

About noontime I reached a village. But I was almost naked and covered with blood and wounds. The villagers thought that I had run away from the government prison, and their hearts melted with pity. They washed the blood from my body, applied balm to my wounds, and brought me food and tea. Out of pity they decided to hide me in their village.

In the middle of the night I heard the galloping of horses. The horsemen asked about me, and I learned that they had been dispatched by the friends. They came in and informed me that the governor had sent twenty horsemen in different directions to find me and assist me to reach a safe destination. They had brought me some money and a cloak. I gave the money to the head of the village, thanked him and the villagers for their generous hospitality, and bade farewell to them. The horsemen told me that we had to reach the city of

Quchán before sunrise. But I was still in great pain, utterly exhausted, and could not ride a horse at great speed. Therefore, they decided to tie me to the horse and make it ride at a gallop until we reached our destination.

We arrived at the house of Mírzá Ḥusayn, and the people of his household, seeing me in that deplorable condition, burst into tears. They wept so bitterly that I could not control my own tears. When we were seated, I told them the whole story and explained that all such events had been foretold in a Tablet I had received from Bahá'u'lláh in which He stated that I would receive religious sanction and punishment.

They informed me that the mob had been aroused to such a frenzy that all the friends and their homes were in danger of attack. They also told me that the Shujá'u'd-Dawlih was furious. He had accused all the divines of conspiring against him. He sent them a message demanding to know why such events had taken place. The 'ulamá proved the worst of liars and the basest of cowards. They answered with the message, "We know nothing about what the people have done."

But the brave governor was not satisfied with this false reply. He dispatched soldiers to their town and ordered them to close the theological school, beat its occupants, and bring them all to his presence. Thirty-five siyyids and mullás were dragged to the governor's house. The Shujá'u'd-Dawlih issued an order to beat them all; it took the whole day. After that they were put in prison.

The governor sent a message to Mírzá Ḥusayn, in whose house I had taken refuge, telling both of us, "You will not be able to withstand the onslaught of the wicked mullás and vicious inhabitants of this town. Before sunrise, come to my house." We went to the governor's house, where we beheld the evildoers of the town who had been beaten.

The news of our visit to see the prisoners went far and wide. Soon more than four hundred people who claimed to be the relatives of the prisoners came to me. They cried and begged me to intercede so that the mullás might be freed. Therefore, I approached the governor and asked him to permit the prisoners to go home. He graciously complied with my request.

But the fire of persecution was ignited everywhere. Soldiers went to the inns and announced that anyone who sheltered me would be severely punished and fined. I was in a room at one such inn when I heard the innkeeper ask the soldiers, "Please tell me what kind of man he is. Is he tall or short; old or young?"

The answer was always the same: "You should not give him shelter."

Upon hearing this, I left the inn and became homeless. Wherever I sought lodging I knew that my hosts would be in serious danger because of me. I wavered between hope and fear—hope of reaching some place where I would not endanger the lives of the friends, and fear of the evil consequences which might be heaped upon the Bahá'í communities in small towns and villages where I stayed. I roamed to the east and west, the north and south, and finally came to Ṭihrán.

Mullá Riḍá, the famous preacher of Ṭihrán, spoke every day in the shah's mosque. There was no topic which would please and excite his followers more than the condemnation of the Bahá'í Faith. He recounted to them all sorts of incredible, profane, and fallacious stories. He even dared to announce that the advent of the promised Qá'im, the Imám Mihdí, would definitely take place in the year 1300 A.H. (circa 1883 A.D.).

It happened that there was an outstanding Bahá'í by the name of Siyyid Mihdí. The governor of Ṭihrán used to show great respect and homage toward him. For example, once when Siyyid Mihdí desired to go out of the governor's room, the governor hastened to the door, bent down, picked up the siyyid's shoes and placed them at his feet. Such a gesture of respect and devotion was unheard of during the reign of the Qájárs, who were absolutely opposed to the Bahá'ís.

On one occasion this siyyid came to Ṭihrán, and many of the friends went to receive him upon his arrival. When I saw the majestic approach of Siyyid Mihdí, I told the friends, "Go to Mullá Riḍá and tell him that his promised Mihdí is here now." For a long time this became a standing joke among the friends. But alas! The same siyyid was soon overcome by his own self and gradually withdrew from the Faith of God, desiring nothing except to acquire material possessions.

In those days, hundreds of Bahá'ís in Ṭihrán were infatuated with this siyyid. But I could see that he manifested nothing but pride and self-importance. I could not bear this situation, so I left Ṭihrán for other provinces.

IN THE CITY OF QUM, I had the pleasure of meeting the Naddaf family. The two Naddaf brothers had agreed to work long hours in order to earn as much money as possible. They spent some of their earnings for their daily living and offered the rest to the Cause of God, as a token of their gratitude for having attained the knowledge and acceptance of such a stupendous Cause. They were illiterate, but it was evident that their hearts had received innate knowledge through the grace of God. The other members of their families were not Bahá'ís, but the brothers did what they could to make them friendly to the Faith. For example, when people like myself would go to their house as guests, the two brothers would go to the market and purchase gifts. Upon returning home, they would go to the women of their household and give them whatever they had purchased, saying, "Our friend has brought these gifts for you." During the same year that I was in their house, they prepared to go to the Holy Land to visit the beloved Master.

Once, Ḥájí Siyyid Javád, a noble, dignified, and illumined believer, left Ṭihrán for Yazd and Kirmán. On his way he stayed in the city of Qum. The two Naddaf brothers found him in one of the inns and brought him some provisions. As they were having dinner together one night, the Naddafs began to talk about the Faith. The siyyid warned them against talking loudly. "Some people may hear and arouse the people to riot against us," he said.

One of the two brothers replied, "You will be on your way home tomorrow. Our other guest will also leave us soon. No one will remain here except us. We are the ones who should be cautious, because the people here know us as Bahá'ís. Therefore, let us avail ourselves of this opportunity to meet you, hear your news, and listen to your exhortations. In this way the people will gradually learn about the Faith.

"Should they stand against us and begin to cause troubles, what shall we do? It is part of God's plan. Through affliction, difficulties, and tests He makes His Cause known. He is the All-Powerful. What can we do? We are the weakest of creatures, the most unknown, and the least significant. Can we go against His overwhelming power?"

The siyyid was astounded by their eloquence and deep understanding. "Remember the days when the Prophet Muḥammad declared His Mission to His compatriots," one of them continued. "The first ones who arrayed themselves against Him were His close relatives, the members of the Quraysh clan. One night they invited the Prophet to their abode and received Him with utmost courtesy, praise, and respect. When seated, one of them very disdainfully addressed Him: 'Our clan is the most noble of Mecca and we have the privilege and honor to be servants of the Ka'bih.[33] Because of this custodianship, we are respected and revered by all the tribes of Arabia. Now, what you proclaim will become the cause of destruction to this shrine and will create such turmoil that our exalted position, rank, and honor will be totally destroyed. Therefore, we request that you forget your claim and have pity on your family, clan, and people. Otherwise you will gain nothing except persecution, poverty, humiliation, and grievous results in this life and in the life to come.'

"When they finished their address, they found Muḥammad in tears. The arrogant members of the Quraysh family took these tears of compassion as a sign of His weakness and compliance with their disgraceful demands. Moved by His tears, they inquired as to the cause. He then opened His mouth and pearls of eternal truth were given them. 'I believe in God, Who is the Ever-watchful, the All-Compelling,' He said. 'I have never claimed anything counter to His will, plan, or desire. He commanded me to rise and say, "I am chosen by Him to be His Messenger." I am a human being with the limitations of a man, but I am held in His grasp. How can I ever disobey the One Who is the King of all Kings and the sole Ruler of this world and the Kingdom above?' "

We all benefited greatly from this deep and meaningful exposition. As they had said, we left the city of Qum for other destinations, and these two illustrious brothers stood steadfast for more than forty years against the cruel onslaught of the most prejudiced inhabitants of that city. Tempestuous opposition created by the oppressors could never shake them. Amidst storms of accusations they cried, "We believe!" and remained unshaken and unmoved. They continued to teach and to receive all the Bahá'ís who passed through Qum.

To SHOW the hazardous conditions under which the early believers lived and served, I would like to tell you another story which took place in the city of Qum. On one of my trips, the same Naddaf brothers told me of a Muslim friend they knew. He was essentially spiritual, upright, and trustworthy, but he would not accept anything which was not sanctioned by the 'ulamá. It was decided to meet this man in a garden far away from the tumult of the town. Our meeting was arranged and our conversation was carried on with mutual love and courtesy. In the course of the conversation, I said something remotely concerned with the Faith. Our friend realized what my purpose was and he kindly said, "What you say is true, but judgment of such matters lies in the hands of the 'ulamá. Let us talk about countries and climates and the customs of tribes and nations."

I asked him, "Is it permissible for you to take a written question to the 'ulamá and request them to give you a concise and proper answer?"

"Yes, if you will kindly write it down."

So I wrote on a piece of paper: "What are the proofs by which we understand that the Qu'rán is the everlasting miracle of the Prophet?" And our naive guest took the written question to the 'ulamá and requested an answer.

When the mullás read this one sentence, they immediately became angry and attacked our friend. They beat him and cursed him and humiliated him. They accused him of being a Bahá'í and tried to imprison him. But this injustice and weakness of the 'ulamá and their inability to answer one simple question awakened this pure-hearted seeker, and he embraced the Faith of God.

THE NEXT STORY took place in the city of Káshán, where there were many Bahá'ís whose profession was weaving. Because during these years there were not many customers for such handwoven goods, the friends were very poor. Jináb-i-Ghulám 'Alí was the most outstanding member of the community. Though not rich, he was always ready to share what he had with the friends and their guests. At his home the favorite dish was a kind of soup to which water could be added when newcomers dropped in unexpectedly. The friends consumed the soup with pieces of bread while the host, who was a well-known humorist, told them jokes and stories. Very often we stayed together in his house until sunrise.

Though poor in material means, the beloved friends of Káshán took care of, protected, and served the poor and destitute, forsaken widows, invalids, and strangers. They were the very embodiment of the verses in the

Qur'án in which the Prophet exhorts His people to always prefer others to their own selves and to sacrifice all to the service of their fellowmen.

In Shíráz I had the honor of meeting three spiritual stars who shone from the horizon of unity. They were as one soul in three bodies. In their commercial dealings they shared profits and losses together, and they carried on this unity in their servitude to the Cause and to the beloved friends. When two of them—Ghulám Ḥusayn and Siyyid 'Alí—passed away, the third, Jináb-i-Dihqán, brought their families under the wing of his care and protection. He looked after the members of these two households as a devoted and affectionate friend and arranged the education of the children on a much higher level than they had enjoyed during the lifetimes of their own fathers. Jináb-i-Dihqán was a standard bearer of the Cause. He sacrificed every atom of his being to the Covenant of God. In addition to inviting me into his house, where I stayed for more than one year and received every day his loving hospitality, he volunteered to pay for my teaching trips. He regularly sent me all the money that I needed during my journeys in Iran.

We heard that Jináb-i-Varqá [34] had been on his way to Shíráz when the soldiers arrested him and took him back to Iṣfahán as a prisoner. One of the Afnán,[35] Siyyid Aḥmad, could not bear to hear about such senseless persecution, which afflicted the friends everywhere. He therefore wrote me a letter and asked me to gather a group of Bahá'ís to go to Russia and lodge complaints against the atrocities inflicted upon the Bahá'ís of Iran. I immediately wrote back and said that this suggestion was against the explicit text of Bahá'u'lláh's teachings. We, as Bahá'ís, must be obedient to our governments and abide by their decisions. Such proposals are wrong, I told him; if the enemies of the Faith learn of this plan, all the Bahá'ís will be in danger, especially people like yourself who are wealthy.

Siyyid Aḥmad wrote back and said, "I knew that my proposal was fraught with danger. Now I will be happy and content if we are all sacrificed in the path of His Faith. It is certain that the news of such sacrifice will be heard by many. Thus the fame of the Cause will spread in all directions."

I then wrote back to him and explained that the people of Bahá should not hope to sacrifice their lives by their own choice or plan. Martyrdom is a bounty which can be obtained only through the grace and pleasure of God.

I CONTINUED my journeys and reached Yazd. There I had the joyous experience of meeting Afnán Kabír, the maternal uncle of the Báb. He bore a great resemblance to the Exalted Báb in both countenance and character. He was known for his honesty and trustworthiness, his kindness and chastity, his charity and generosity. Though people knew him as one of the followers of the Faith, he remained the most trusted and respected individual in the province of Yazd. The 'ulamá and the government officials respected him to such a degree that the most difficult and frustrating cases were referred to him and his judgment sought and invariably obeyed. All the other Afnán lived under his shadow. Many believers were attracted to the Faith by his spiritual attainments.

The Afnán of Yazd and Shíráz received a Tablet from Bahá'u'lláh in which He expressed the desire that the friends should settle in 'Ishqábád, Russia. Two master masons arose to answer the call of their Lord. They set out for 'Ishqábád with the intention of building shops, houses, and an inn for the Afnán. I accompanied them, hoping that I could be of some service to the Faith.

On our way we reached Fárán where the illustrious Mír Muḥammad had his residence. He and his large family had been the pivot of affairs in that town, and thus the friends were well protected and lived in peace under the vigilant eye of this veteran general of the Army of Light. It was here that I received the answer to my letter sent from Shíráz. In this Tablet, Bahá'u'lláh praised the sacrificial spirit and devotion of Siyyid Aḥmad, but to his aforementioned plan He definitely said, "No." As to myself, He instructed me that it would not be wise for me to go to 'Ishqábád. The two masons were encouraged to go there, settle, and serve the Faith. I was told that I was also forbidden to go to Iṣfahán or Ṭihrán. Beyond this, the believers advised me not to go to Yazd or Shíráz because I was too well known in those places, and my presence might cause disturbances.

I wrote back to the Holy Land and said, "My God, what should I do? Ṭihrán, Iṣfahán, and 'Ishqábád are forbidden by you, and Shíráz and Yazd by your steadfast servants." I was at a loss for what to do. The doors of all the provinces were closed to me. I wandered around the province of Khurásán, existing only by the generosity of the Afnán. I knew that I had no way out of this dilemma except to turn my face toward 'Akká and leave Iran for His holy presence.

Since one of the faithful maidservants of the Cause who lived in Ṭihrán had written to Bahá'u'lláh asking that she might marry me, the Blessed Perfection ordered me to travel to Ṭihrán to be married. Permission to go to the Holy Land came in the next Tablet. For the next fourteen or fifteen years that faithful maidservant who was inflamed with the love of Bahá'u'lláh served me with humility and selflessness. Her devoted services to me were so great that I am ashamed when I mention them.

I set out for the Holy Land, and part of the journey was by sea. On board ship I met someone from 'Akká who constantly talked of 'Abbás Effendi and His unique character. I told him that I knew that He had many followers in Iran, but asked him to tell me more. He was encouraged to relate more stories about 'Abdu'l-Bahá. He praised Him so highly that I eventually told him, "Now, I must go to 'Akká and meet this exalted person."

After disembarking in the Holy Land, this same man hastened to 'Abdu'l-Bahá before me and said, "I have talked about the Faith to a Persian and he will be coming here to visit you. Surely he will become a Bahá'í!"

BEFORE ENTERING the presence of the Blessed Beauty, I prepared myself for a great spiritual feast. I repeated in my mind and heart: "This is the day foretold by all the Prophets of God. This is the town praised and exalted by David. This is the plain of Sharon coveted by all the Holy Ones of the past. Now you are here with the burden of your sins and shortcomings." When my eager eyes fell upon the countenance of my Lord, I was so overwhelmed that I could not describe my feelings to the friends. I was indeed like a dumb person who has a sweet dream and is powerless to describe it.

Bahá'u'lláh asked me about the friends in Iran, and He granted me the courage and the power to speak in His presence. "The beloved friends, though from widely different backgrounds, having grown up with different ideas, beliefs, and degrees of understanding, are united in one thing," I said, "and that is to win the pleasure of God. Confined in prisons, kept in chains, beset by perpetual hardships and persecutions, they remain firm and steadfast so that the Ancient Beauty will be pleased with them."

ONE NIGHT the beloved Master spoke about Mullá 'Alí-Ján. When I was traveling in the districts of Mázindarán, I had the honor of meeting this great and illumined soul. I discovered that Mullá 'Alí-Ján had taught more than five hundred people in Máhfu-rújak and its surrounding areas. Besides bringing them into the Cause, he had educated them and deepened them. He had instructed the women to cover their hair and to dress modestly. He had taught the men to dress neatly and to be meticulously clean. It was absolutely forbidden for them to use vulgar or profane words. He instructed that in each house a special room be suitably furnished for prayer. Upon their return home from a day's work, men and women alike would wash, change their clothes, and perform their prayers. After dinner the friends would be called to gather in one of the houses for a meeting to discuss Bahá'í matters. He had selected a few to teach and educate the other believers. His wife and his three nephews helped him in these efforts by transcribing the Tablets and chanting them with melodious voices in the meetings. The Bahá'ís of Máhfurújak were so well trained that, although they were all well known, the 'ulamá could not find any reason to complain about their behavior.

Mullá 'Alí-Ján was so deeply enthralled by the love of God that whenever he heard any Tablet read at the gatherings of the friends, he would take these words as a call inviting him to return to his Creator. Often he said to himself, "'Alí! 'Alí! 'Alí! Are you still sitting here? Are you still living comfortably? Your Lord has written to you. Why don't you hasten into the arena of sacrifice? Why don't you raise your voice in His praise?"

The time came when the same Mullá 'Alí-Ján was taken captive because of a decree issued by the 'ulamá. He was taken in chains to Ṭihrán and brought to the house of Kámrán Mírzá, a high official. Kámrán Mírzá approached him and said, "I have brought you good news! If you just tell me that you know nothing about this Cause, you will immediately be set free and allowed to return to your home and family. Furthermore, I will grant you a regular salary, special clothes adorned with the royal emblem, and a title from the shah. Please have pity upon yourself and upon your children."

"I will never agree to such a humiliating transaction," 'Alí-Ján replied. "I will not barter my religion for gold, nor exchange eternal life for this ephemeral world. Tribulation in the path of God is to me far more exalted than anything in this mundane life."

He was immediately put in heavy chains and sent to one of the squares of Ṭihrán to be killed. Under the burden of those heavy fetters, he walked so quickly that the executioners could not keep up with him. Many people who witnessed his execution became attracted to the Faith because of his courage, his inner joy, and his complete assurance.

Mullá 'Alí-Ján's wife, 'Alavíyyih Khánum, also had her share of suffering. After the martyrdom of her husband, she was arrested by the governor. He addressed her, saying, "How dare you claim to be Fáṭimih, the daughter of the Prophet Muḥammad!"

"I have never claimed that," was her courageous reply. "But now that you have made me a captive, I feel certain that I belong to her family." Although she was only twenty-three years of age when she lost her husband, she never accepted another marriage. She expended her youth and all that she had in traveling and serving the Cause. She had the honor of attaining the presence of the Master.

THE SPIRITUAL transformation experienced by those who have attained the presence of Bahá'u'lláh is so far above limited human experience that it cannot be described. It is that Paradise which is said never to have been seen by mortal eyes, nor experienced by earthly senses. The experience is like a tempestuous ocean, each wave of which brings forth pearls of beauty. Yet the waters of this ocean are so blissful that one does not even want to swim, but only wishes to be drowned in its ecstasy. This unbelievable joy often comes and passes like lightning. It is only granted to a few through a special bounty of the Lord, and then it will be manifested only as strongly as their spiritual capacity will allow.

Once I requested to be in Bahá'u'lláh's room when He was revealing Tablets. This request met with His approval. As I entered His room, I heard streams of words sweeping along in a torrential flow from His lips. It seemed that the atmosphere, the floor, the walls, and every atom in the room was filled with perfume. Only those who have had this indescribable experience can ever imagine what I mean. The flow of revelation continued for about five minutes. Then Bahá'u'lláh said to me, "You have on several occasions been here when the revelation of Tablets has taken place. Should the people of the whole world wish to be present and hear the words of revelation, We would permit them. But since We have approved courtesy and ordained it upon men, we are reluctant to display this power publicly."

The story is told that the brutal Shaykh Muḥammad-Báqir who was responsible for the martyrdom of so many Bahá'ís and whom Bahá'u'lláh named "The Wolf" because of his evil plots, once shouted from his pulpit, "Translate the chapter of the Qu'rán in which the Prophet Muḥammad proclaims that God is one, has always existed, and can never be born. Give this to the Bahá'ís who have taken Bahá'u'lláh as their God."

When the Ancient Beauty heard this, He said that Moses had heard the call of "I am your God" from a burning bush. Why not from a man?

FOR A LONG TIME I carried the desire to prostrate myself at the feet of Bahá'u'lláh. Once I was admitted to His room as He was pacing the floor. When He came toward me, I flattened myself against the wall. As He walked away, I followed Him one or two steps in the hope of fulfilling my heart's desire. But then He turned, and I retreated and stood meekly against the wall.

"What is the matter?" He said, with a heavenly smile. "I see that you are going back and forth." Then He stretched forth His hand and commanded me, "Stay where you are!" Though my wish was not fulfilled, the movement of His hand and that smile of pleasure brought me immeasurable joy.

ON THIS PILGRIMAGE also, when I was asked to depart, I requested that I be permitted to remain two more weeks. Bahá'u'lláh again asked for a guarantee. I immediately replied, "The Master!" since we all knew that the Master's wish would be done. That evening I was admitted to the room of the Blessed Beauty where He told me, "Stay one month more. Your Guarantee is great, beloved, and precious. So you may stay more."

Then He continued, "In the days when We lived in Baghdád, We used to go to a coffeehouse where We would meet friends, strangers, and all sorts of people. This was the means by which the Word of God could be heard, and many souls were led into the Cause. But in Adrianople, and here in 'Akká, it is the Master who performs these services. He must face the same hardships which We faced previously. In Baghdád We were not imprisoned, and the fame of the Cause was not even a hundredth part of what it is today. Also, the enemies of the Cause were not as many or as powerful as they are now. In Adrianople We met many people, but in the Most Great Prison, We seldom receive visitors who are not believers. The burden of all these affairs has fallen upon the shoulders of the Master. To provide Us with some peace and comfort, He has made Himself Our shield, and thus He sees to Our affairs both with the government and with the people. He first prepared for Us the house at Mazra'ih, and then He procured this Mansion in Bahjí. He is so devoted to His services and so intensely occupied that sometimes weeks pass by and He cannot come here to visit Us. While We consort with the friends and reveal Tablets, He is immersed in the toils and troubles of the world."

When I was permitted to come again into Bahá'u'lláh's presence, He said, "The utterances of the Most Great Branch ['Abdu'l-Bahá] and His power are now concealed. Later it will be seen how He, singly and alone, will raise the banner of the Faith in the world. He will gather all mankind under the Tabernacle of peace and submission." This was, of course, only the gist of His words, so far as I can remember them.

Bahá'u'lláh was usually in His room in the Mansion of Bahjí. From there He could see 'Abdu'l-Bahá as He approached the Mansion from 'Akká. When He would catch sight of Him, He would invariably ask all those in His presence to go out to meet Him.

One day Bahá'u'lláh was very sad. His sadness was caused by the behavior of a few of the believers who lived in His household. In great sorrow He said, "Were it possible, We would recommend that the pilgrims who enter the city of ‘Akká go directly to the presence of the Most Great Branch, listen to Him, then meet some of the steadfast believers, and immediately afterwards leave ‘Akká and return to their homes. This would be most conducive to their spiritual development. The reason is this: In the Master’s presence the friends are not subjected to tainted human thoughts and deeds. All they experience is heavenly sanctity. If the people would open their eyes, they would see clearly the difference between the heavenly perfections of the Master and the human frailties and faults of others. Then, even if they witness odious deeds committed in My household, they will only utter words of praise about the greatness and patience of the True One Who is glorious, mighty, and compassionate. We are aware of their false words and lies. We know. But We must remain silent and cover their sins. Unfortunately, the liars think that We do not know the truth.”

A TAILOR by the name of Muḥammad-‘Alí came on pilgrimage. He had a good character and a happy disposition, and he was endowed with quick understanding. He often circumambulated the Mansion of Bahjí. When he came to meet the friends, he would make them happy with his beautiful stories. Once he sent me a letter in which he related that a very famous mystic leader had said, “O God! If I hear Thee calling me only once ‘My servant,’ I will ascend to heaven.” He told me that he had often walked around the gardens near the Mansion of Bahjí and felt immense joy. But never had he heard those sweet words.

I sent a letter to Bahá'u'lláh about this pilgrim, and we received a wonderful Tablet in which He calls each one of us "My servant" not one, but nine times. In the Islamic traditions we had read the famous saying, "Should the people approach Him only one yard, He will hasten to them by miles." Now we saw the fulfillment of this promise.

Now there remained only three nights until the end of my pilgrimage, and I was summoned to the presence of Bahá'u'lláh. He spoke of His exiles and emphasized the fact that should the people ponder carefully on these different stages of His banishment, they would know that every step had been taken according to the Will of God. "The hand of God is over all, and His might and power overwhelm the worlds of creation. Consider the case of those persons who, fearing the loss of their temporal powers, condemned Us to the Most Great Prison. Where are they now? What has befallen each and every one of them? God brought them down from their places and consigned them to their graves. Their names are never mentioned. But your Lord is established in this Mansion through the power of God, His might, and His sovereignty."

He then asked someone to chant parts of the two Tablets addressed to the sultan of the Ottoman Empire and to the shah of Persia. After that, the pilgrims were dismissed.

During our dinner someone brought sweets sent to us by Bahá'u'lláh. He also sent a message concerning me: "Tell him to eat the sweets and say to himself, 'I must go home.'" This time I got ready to go and did not plan to ask the beloved Master to intervene on my behalf or to guarantee me. The sweet memory of His loving wit that I should tell myself, "I must go home," remains fresh in my heart, and even more as I surrender my will to that of God.

The next day we had torrential rains. In the afternoon of that same day, I went to see Him. The moment I entered His room, He said, "It seems that you expect the rain to intercede for you." This tender joke helped to change all my despair into joy. When I returned to the Pilgrim House and reported my interview to the friends, they were all of the opinion that the next day there would again be rain, and that Bahá'u'lláh would not send me away.

But the day dawned with splendid sunshine, and I went to His room in the Mansion of Bahjí. He spoke about teaching. He said: "A kindly approach and loving behavior toward the people are the first requirements for teaching the Cause. The teacher must carefully listen to whatever a person has to say—even though his talk may consist only of vain imaginings and blind repetitions of the opinions of others. One should not resist or engage in argument. The teacher must avoid disputes which will end in stubborn refusal or hostility, because the other person will feel overpowered and defeated. Therefore, he will be more inclined to reject the Cause. One should rather say, 'Maybe you are right, but kindly consider the question from this other point of view.' Consideration, respect, and love encourage people to listen and do not force them to respond with hostility. They are convinced because they see that your purpose is not to defeat them, but to convey truth, to manifest courtesy, and to show forth heavenly attributes. This will encourage the people to be fair. Their spiritual natures will respond, and, by the bounty of God, they will find themselves recreated.

"Consider the way in which the Master teaches the people. He listens very carefully to the most hollow and senseless talk. He listens so intently that the speaker says to himself, 'He is trying to learn from me.' Then the Master gradually and very carefully, by means that the other person does not perceive, puts him on the right path and endows him with a fresh power of understanding."

When the final moment approached and I bade farewell to my Beloved, He approached the door and whispered in my ear, "I have entrusted you to the hands of the Master." Though these words were spoken with the utmost sweetness, and were a sign of His sublime consideration and love, they filled my heart with dark clouds of sorrow. They seemed to me to indicate clearly His imminent departure from this world.

Next I went to 'Akká, to the presence of the Master. There was no end to His love. He had written a letter to Bahá'u'lláh requesting that I be permitted to stay, even outside the city of 'Akká, because the sea had been rough and agitated. His letter had been returned with one sentence on the top: "It is better for him to go; God is the Protector—rest assured."

FROM 'AKKÁ I went to Haifa and boarded a ship bound for Constantinople. After a short stay in that city I went on to Baku, in Russian Caucasia, and from there to Ṭihrán.

In Ṭihrán I learned that Muslims had attacked the friends in Ishtihárd, confiscated their property, beaten both men and women, imprisoned them, and destroyed their houses. More than fifty of these believers were now in Ṭihrán, and they gathered together to consult about this situation. They decided to send a petition to the court of the shah asking for justice. Since they heard that I had been in the Holy Land, they asked to meet me in order to hear about the One in Whose path they had sacrificed their homes, their property, and their loved ones, and for Whom they were willing to offer up their own lives.

At this time it was not safe to hold large Bahá'í meetings in Ṭihrán. Therefore, after consultation, we agreed that every night only five of them would come, accompanied by the Hand of the Cause Mullá 'Alí-Akbar. We made ready to receive five, but at the appointed hour fifty of them entered my room. Our joy knew no bounds. We chanted Tablets and prayers. We spoke of Bahá'u'lláh and consulted about their persecutions. Four hours after sunset, thinking that there would not be enough food for the more than fifty people who had gathered, I refrained from inviting them for dinner and they all departed.

When my wife learned of this, she became very sad. With tears in her eyes, she rebuked me. "I have prepared bread, cheese, and meat for more than fifty people," she said. "These are the ones whose houses have been plundered in the path of God. Their families are dispersed because of their love for Bahá'u'lláh. Now, homeless and unsheltered as they are, they come to our humble home. What answer will we have if God asks us, 'Why did you send them away unfed?' "

It was only then that I realized what a grave error I had committed. It is true that we must be prudent, but in this case I had been most uncharitable. To satisfy my wife and to make her dear heart happy and contented, we agreed that all of them would come again to our home, in groups of six, for dinner.

NOT LONG AFTER THAT I was instructed to go to Iṣfahán. I reached there when the families of the two illustrious believers, the King of Martyrs and the Beloved of Martyrs,[36] were preparing to go to the Holy Land. These dear friends were constantly in trouble. The governor and the 'ulamá, through their evil agents, were always ready to heap fresh persecutions upon them. Their departure from the tumultuous town of Iṣfahán seemed impossible.

The dreadful memory of the days when the force of hatred was set loose in Iṣfahán, and swallowed these two brothers in its flames, was still vivid in their minds. They were afraid that the same fate would befall the remaining members of their family. But their longing to reach His presence was stronger than their caution. Eventually their love overcame their fear, and they courageously made their way homeward—to the home of their hearts and souls. When they reached the Holy Land, the bounties they received were beyond measure. They were invited to remain in His presence for one year.

After their departure for the Holy Land, the sleeping giant awoke, and the inhabitants of Iṣfahán threatened to tear down their houses, plunder their riches, and cut the pilgrims themselves to pieces as soon as they might return. Anxiety and fear prevailed everywhere, and the other believers in the city lived in perpetual anxiety.

Eventually I wrote to the Holy Land, explained the situation, and suggested that the pilgrims stay in Ṭihrán for some months until, by the grace of God, this consuming fire might be extinguished. The reply was prompt and decisive. In a Tablet, Bahá'u'lláh assured the friends that the pilgrims would return safely. He revealed a prayer for them to chant upon their arrival home.

When our friends returned to Iṣfahán, they were accorded great respect by the people. Many of the 'ulamá and the notables came to their houses to welcome them home.

During this period, Mírzá Abu'l-Faḍl [37] blessed the soil of Iṣfahán with his presence. As he had been a student in Iṣfahán some years before, many of the divines and students of theology knew him well. But when they met him again, they discovered that this man was not the same Mírzá Abu'l-Faḍl whom they had known as a student in their theological schools. Then he was but a drop. Now they discovered that he had become an ocean. One of the famous teachers of the town, after visiting him, declared, "If all the erudite leaders of our time surrounded Mírzá Abu'l-Faḍl, he would be a giant among pygmies. He is truly unique to our age, and eclipses any one of the 'ulamá in oration, in reasoning, and in his ability to explain philosophical questions."

ON ONE OF MY TRIPS to Iṣfahán I arrived during the night and went directly to the house of one of the friends. It was almost midnight. The owner of the house prepared tea for me, but I saw signs of sorrow and anxiety on his face. When I inquired as to the reason, he said, "Yesterday they killed Mullá As͟hraf. And now they are looking for me." I asked him to tell me more.

"Some days ago, As͟hraf related a dream to us. In his dream he had seen the Báb, Who summoned him to His exalted presence. Immediately he found that he could fly. He began to soar higher and higher to reach Him. As he approached the Báb, his cloak fell off. When he reached His presence, the Báb said, 'Look!' He looked, and found all the people illumined and united, with the light of love emanating from each. They were all singing songs in praise of the Greatest Name.

"When he related this dream, Ashraf told us that he regarded it as a clear indication of his return to his Lord. He felt that this would take place very soon."

Two or three days passed. He met a man, a wolf in sheep's clothing, who pretended to be a true seeker after truth. Ashraf spoke about the Faith to him on four consecutive nights. Then the "seeker" invited him to have tea with him in one of the schools of theology. Friends of Ashraf who knew this "seeker" urged him not to accept the invitation. They warned that this man was a Judas Iscariot. In answer to their warnings, Ashraf said, "I leave my affairs in the hands of God." And he went. The moment he stepped into the school, three or four soldiers arrested him and dragged him to the seat of the governor. When he reached there, it was night and he was placed in prison.

In the morning the people of Iṣfahán saw a cross raised in the public square of their city. But they did not know why it had been erected. Ashraf was brought to the governor's house. Although frail in body, he had been placed in chains. His dignified demeanor and his tranquil appearance so impressed the members of the government that even some of the princes arose to intervene on his behalf. "Do not stain your hands with the blood of this old man," they warned. But their appeal fell on deaf ears. They raised this noble soul on the cross, but it broke. And so the day ended and Ashraf was returned to prison.

On the second day, the crowd gathered once more in the same square. All the notables pleaded on Ashraf's behalf even more fervently than before. They insisted that the murder of this old man would be an evil omen for the governor. But the governor remained adamant. Finally he shouted, "Let the 'ulamá gather and debate with him. Should his killing seem wrong and unjust, may God keep him safe from the fury of Áqá Najafí."

On the third day, the 'ulamá assembled in the presence of the governor. Two thousand people stood waiting for the arrival of As͟hraf. He was brought in with heavy chains. They asked him questions, and he gave eloquent and courageous answers.

The 'ulamá ordered him to recant his faith. He declared, "I abhor all lies, all deviations, and all false claims." But they were not satisfied.

"Exonerate yourself by cursing the names of the founders of the Bahá'í religion," Najafí demanded.

"The cursing of names is forbidden in the Qu'rán, even to denounce the gods of heathens," was As͟hraf's firm answer. "I believe in Islám. I greeted you with 'Salám 'Alaykum.' I am a mujtahid like yourselves; I know that it is the duty of every true Muslim to investigate the fundamental principles of his own religion." Many of the notables and dignitaries became disgusted with these unfair proceedings and so left the meeting in anger.

Najafí became more furious than ever and shouted, "Let the people come in and bear witness to the fact that this man teaches the Bábí Faith!"

As͟hraf immediately answered, "It is very clear that people recruited from the market or the streets who come in and find me in chains will surely accuse me of whatever you wish. Remove the chains and then bring the people and have them point to who is guilty." But they would not agree. At this point there was another exodus of government officials; even some of the 'ulamá left the meeting. Prince 'Abbás G͟hulí Mírzá became very angry. He stood up and as he left the room said, "They are unjustly killing an old man, and yet they claim to be the religious leaders of the town."

None of these remarks quenched the thirst of Áqá Najafí for the blood of Mullá Ashraf. He issued a decree that he must be put to death.

Though Ashraf was old, he hastened toward his cross so quickly that the soldiers could not overtake him. Upon his arrival at the cross, he kissed it and said, "We are of God and to Him shall we return." His highest wish was fulfilled, and his name became immortalized in one of the Tablets of Bahá'u'lláh. In this Tablet He says that the city of lovers became filled with love and exultation because one of the precious jewels decided to make its way back to His eternal treasure house, that one of His lovers hastened and attained the presence of his Beloved. The Exalted Pen expressed intense distress about the ignorant mob and the proud 'ulamá who remained unmoved at the sight of such a wondrous sacrifice.

AFTER THESE DREADFUL DAYS, the friends did not find it wise for me to prolong my stay in Iṣfahán. I left for other parts. For many months I journeyed through different provinces of Persia, staying longer in Kirmán where many strong and malignant enemies of the Cause were living. They had one, and only one, track to follow—to disprove and refute the teachings of the Faith. This they did constantly by every means which their wicked hearts could devise. Sometimes they forged tablets which they showed to people to discourage them from investigating the Faith. Association with such people was even more difficult than the tortures of prison.

In Khurásán I had the pleasure of meeting the lion-hearted Faḍil-i-Furúghí. He was a treasure of learning and zeal. Many a time I proposed to him that such a staunch upholder of the Cause should leave his small town, travel around Persia, and impart to the friends his knowledge and love. The day came when he began his journeys. No sooner did he step into the arena of sacrifice and service outside his village than his fame went far and wide. Eventually he became a target for the jealousy and malevolence of the 'ulamá, who devised the most cunning plots against him. Repeatedly the most outstanding members of the clergy decreed for him imprisonment, exile, and death. He became a wanderer and eventually was captured and put in chains. His life was in such danger that none of the friends had the slightest hope of his survival. However, after his release from prison, it seemed that some mysterious force protected him and enabled him to achieve great success in his teaching trips. The meetings held in his presence vibrated with his spiritual ardor. In one Tablet 'Abdu'l-Bahá calls him "The Commander of the Great Army." He made a pilgrimage and returned to Persia with renewed courage, enthusiasm, and fervor.

I also had the honor of visiting the town of Bushrúyih, in Khurásán, the home of Mullá Ḥusayn. When I arrived there, I felt strong spiritual reverberations. It was as if the soil, the water, even the air itself vibrated with divine favors. The whole atmosphere seemed perfumed with the love of the Merciful. It was my joy and honor to visit the sister and nephew of Mullá Ḥusayn.

As the chosen ones were plentiful, so the enemies of the Cause were also many in number. They emerged with fanatic hatred whenever a stranger came to visit the small groups of solitary believers who had no share of life except bitter suffering. The enemies of the Cause were like wild beasts who sharpened their teeth and claws, waiting to pounce on the defenseless Bahá'ís scattered in isolated parts of the country.

My stay lasted one month. People gathered in large numbers to listen to the Writings and to listen to me speak of the Faith. After a while we learned that Muslims were joining forces against the small band of believers. Every morning and every evening we heard the voice of the imám from the top of the minaret of the mosque saying, "Islam is dead. Heresy! Heresy! The people's faith is dead. Where is our religion? What has happened to our faith?"

I wrote to the leading mujtahid of the town and invited him to come to our meetings so that we could debate openly. I said that some government officials would also be asked to attend to witness the debate. This challenge quieted him effectively, and the fire subsided.

I can never forget one gifted woman by the name of Rúhá. She had never been to school, but she was the pride of her sex. She was a heroic soul who, because of her audacious deeds, became known to the shah and his ministers. She was a living Ṭáhirih of those days. A weaver of cloth, her income was scanty, but whatever she earned she spent in traveling around to proclaim the name of Bahá'u'lláh. Her manners, her detachment, and her enterprising spirit are examples to be emulated by every aspiring teacher of the Cause.

In Ṭabas I met a very just and benevolent governor. He was known as 'Imádu'l-Mulk. He was fair and just to all his subjects. Under his rule all were taken care of and protected against ill-wishers. As a young man, he had met Bahá'u'lláh in Iraq, and he mentioned this very often. He had a pocketknife Bahá'u'lláh had given him, which he kept wrapped in a beautiful piece of velvet. He was very proud of the fact that he had had the opportunity of being in His presence.

When he passed away, his son inherited his father's title and position. In his love for the Cause, this son, who was now the governor, even went further than his father. He chose a very beautiful building as the place where the Bahá'í meetings were to be held. There was no end to the love and kindness he showed to the believers. Because of him many important people from the surrounding area became Bahá'ís. He was attracted to the Cause by the fundamental principles of the Faith and by the absence of a special ruling class of clergy. He very much admired the teaching that any controversy among the friends should be removed by referring the matter to the appointed and authorized Interpreter of the Word of God.

In Yazd and in many other provinces of Persia, I found that the distinguished behavior of all the Afnán had won the admiration, wonder, and praise of all who knew them. The seeds sown and watered by the blood of martyrs had grown under the sunshine of the love of these illustrious relatives of the Báb. "They are perfect in everying," people would say. "What a pity that they are Bahá'ís."

When I was in Yazd, I lived in the house of Jináb-i-Afnán. During the summer, because of the intense heat, people would sleep on their roofs. Early one morning, when I descended from the roof, I found Afnán sitting immersed in thought. Because of the deep sadness on his face, I knew that something serious had happened. I did not dare to approach him, since I was still in my sleeping garment and not suitably dressed to attend the presence of such a venerable person. He withdrew, but sent a sealed envelope to me. When I opened it, I found the Tablet of 'Abdu'l-Bahá announcing the ascension of Bahá'u'lláh.

I was so stunned that I could not even cry. The friends gradually gathered in the house of the Afnán. They were so stricken with grief that no one talked. In the midst of this intense sorrow and bewilderment, Jináb-i-Afnán joined us. He wept openly, and all wept with him. He addressed us, saying, "It was decreed that He would one day rid Himself of the endless suffering of this world. It was written that He would one day return to the Source of His glory. Praise be to God that He has left His sorrow-filled friends One Who will guide us. This is no less a person than the 'Mystery of God.' [38] We must hold fast to the hem of His mercy and arise to serve the Cause of God and be His true servants, sacrificing all that we have to uphold our beloved Faith."

After hearing these consoling words, we again read the Tablet of 'Abdu'l-Bahá and decided to hold memorial meetings for nine consecutive days and nights where all the friends would gather together.

The news of His ascension spread everywhere and,

though the population of Persia was at that time in the grip of a merciless attack of cholera, the people made merry and rejoiced and ridiculed the Bahá'ís.

A week after the news of His ascension had reached us, the friends received a copy of the Kitáb-i-'Ahd (The Book of the Covenant). Emphatically and explicitly, He had appointed the beloved Master as the sole Interpreter of His Word. When the friends received this great news, they were calmed, and, with hearts full of hope, they arose to raise the banner of servitude and uphold it with their utmost strength.

THE MINISTRY of 'Abdu'l-Bahá began so vigorously that Bahá'í communities everywhere were overwhelmed. Letters from the Master poured into every village, town, and country like the drops of the rains of spring. The friends were cheered and enamored by His life-giving words. Whoever received a Tablet would make many copies and send them as precious gifts to friends throughout the length and breadth of the East. This opened a new field of activity, that of regular and informative correspondence amongst all the believers.

'Abdu'l-Bahá explained to the Bahá'ís that the physical body of the Prophet of God is like a cloud which covers the sun and which prevents its rays from reaching the earth. Because of their physical limitations, the Prophets of God must live by the rules of physical existence. For this reason, many people are tested. They will say, "What kind of Prophet is He? He sleeps and eats and walks the streets like everyone else." But when the cloud is removed, the rays of the sun reach the people directly, and the whole of creation is resuscitated by their life-giving light.

The friends became aware of their opportunities and bounties. Therefore, they arose in unprecedented numbers to proclaim the Faith and teach the Cause. Gradually, more enthusiasm, unity, and activity developed on every level of Bahá'í life. In a short time lethargy, indifference, and coolness were replaced by intense teaching activities.

Such manifestations of zeal and ardor encouraged me also to act. At the urging of the Afnán, I wrote an open letter to the 'ulamá proclaiming the truth of this Cause. I then began fresh teaching tours in the days of the Covenant.

WHILE I WAS in Ábádih I received a parcel from the Holy Land. It contained eighty-one Tablets written by 'Abdu'l-Bahá. But they came with unusual instructions: "Do not read the Tablets. Choose eighteen believers. As you meet them, write their names on the Tablets and give them away. Do this also in Iṣfahán, Bavánát, and Yazd. Write the name of anyone you choose. You may also send the Tablets to some recipients, if you do not meet them in person."

When I completed the task, I learned that whoever received one of the Master's Tablets found in it an expression responding to his own deepest longings. The fame of this event went everywhere. An Englishman who was the head of the telegraph office of Ábádih heard of this extraordinary occurrence. He said, "It is very strange for me to learn of the spiritual powers of a human being. I wonder how He knew the secrets of these people's souls. The character and perfections of these believers are testimonies to the divine education they receive from Him." This gentleman openly affirmed his belief in the Faith.[39]

I WENT TO IṢFAHÁN, where I met Jináb-i-Vazír. He was the most outstanding person in that district. The finances of the province were under his jurisdiction, and practically everyone in the area knew that he and his family were Bahá'ís. Though the governor knew him better than anyone else, and knew that he was a follower of the Faith, he had absolute confidence in him. Shaykh Najafí, whose thirst for the blood of the Bahá'ís was never quenched, kept silent about Vazír. If he said anything about him, it was in praise. Jináb-i-Vazír treated the shaykh like a hungry wolf. Every now and then he would send him gifts, and this would appease him temporarily.

Ardistán was the home of Jináb-i-Fatḥ-i-A'zam. I had visited him several times, and each time I had witnessed the wonderful signs of courage and steadfastness in him and in his son, Shaháb. This family and that of Jináb-i-Rafí'á were the pillars of the Cause in those regions. There were many Bahá'ís in this town, and most of them lived in one neighborhood. Because of the shining example of these two families, all of the believers were strong and firm in the Covenant.

My tours of Ardistán, Iṣfahán, and the surrounding areas became so fruitful that they enraged Shaykh Najafí. He called for a general meeting in the Mosque of the Shah. When the hall was packed, he ascended the pulpit and began: "O faithful Muslims! To protect Islam is a duty incumbent upon every Muslim. We really did not do enough in the past to eradicate this misguided community of Bábís. Our only consolation was the belief that the one who called himself Bahá'u'lláh and led many people astray would die one day. Then his cause would be forgotten, like those of all false claimants of the past.

"Now we have learned that he has a son who in every respect is more learned and more audacious in the propagation of his religion than his father. He has risen with such might and power that he will soon eradicate Islam and will impose a tax on all Muslims.

"The shah and his government captured, imprisoned, tortured, and killed as many followers of this false religion as they could. Many of them were expelled from the country. But now we see that the government is inactive. Therefore, it is your duty to arise and kill every Bahá'í by every means in your power. We pray that God will aid you and assist you. You must cleanse the country of this hated community. This will be considered as your greatest service to Islam, and your reward will be paradise, where spacious mansions, beautiful angels, and all that your hearts desire are awaiting you."

In every community there are people who are eager to riot and wreak destruction. Such people, once aroused by the religious leaders, consider the worst crimes as acts of piety. This was particularly true in this case, when they could freely attack and kill Bahá'ís, as well as plunder and loot their property. When the believers, who had no means of defense, heard of the attacks of Shaykh Najafí, they could only raise their hands and their eyes to their Lord and beseech His protection.

It happened that the head of the telegraph office, in accordance with his duty, immediately informed the government in Ṭihrán of the way in which Najafí had incited the people to religious persecution. A cable soon reached Iṣfahán from the court of the shah ordering a stop to all such harrassment. Thus the friends remained unmolested.

THERE WAS A PAPER by the name of *Akhtar* which was printed and published in Constantinople. Some of the believers subscribed to it. In one of its issues, news was read that some of the members of Bahá'u'lláh's family had united against the beloved Master. We also heard reports of this kind from some of the foreign embassies. Such things were beyond our imagining, so we denied every such report. We knew that the editor of *Akhtar* was a very obstinate enemy of the Cause and had connections with the Azalís; therefore, we discounted the reports as mere slander.

For a long time I continued to travel from village to village and from town to town. Wherever I went I found the believers faithful to the Cause and actively engaged in teaching. Upon entering Ṭihrán, I received a Tablet from the beloved Master in which He instructed me to continue my travels and urge the friends to remain firm in the Covenant of God, lest they might be innocently entrapped in the deceitful plans of some ambitious souls. This Tablet was a clear indication that there were those near to Him who would pursue their own selfish aims rather than obey the One Bahá'u'lláh had appointed as the Center of His Covenant.

My sorrow knew no bounds when I learned of the activities of Jamál in Ṭihrán. I knew him very well. He had always thought of himself as supreme over all the friends. He would use every means to gain leadership in the Bahá'í community. After the ascension of Bahá'u'-

lláh, he went to the Holy Land without first requesting permission from the Master. After he returned, he no longer hid his ambitions. All the evil thoughts and plans which he used to hint at, he now openly discussed with the friends. But he always embroidered them in the hypocritical design of steadfastness to the Covenant and service to the Master.

From the time that Bahá'u'lláh had been in Adrianople, Javád-i-Qazvíní had always been my connection for sending and receiving correspondence from the Holy Household. Now he wrote a secret letter to me from the Holy Land in which he gave me three instructions. He said that: (1) in my letters to 'Abdu'l-Bahá, or those that I might write on behalf of others, I should never use the phrase, "May I be sacrificed for Thee," or other terms of high respect. Rather, letters should be addressed in the ordinary way. (2) I should not begin my correspondence with prayers. (3) I should never refer to "The Branch," but always say, "The Branches." [40]

This letter was another indication for me that plots in opposition to 'Abdu'l-Bahá were underway in the Holy Land. Since I had seen signs of arrogance and sacrilege from Javád before, I supposed that Jamál and Javád were secretly opposing the Master. Therefore, I suspected that the letter had been written without authorization. I wrote back objecting to all three of the instructions and setting forth my reasons. I added that if these were orders from 'Abdu'l-Bahá, I wanted to receive them in a letter written by His own hand; and if not, I never wanted to receive another letter from Javád. Since I received no answer, I was sure that the birds of night had begun to gather.

It never occurred to me that the chief mover of all these intrigues could possibly be the half brother of the Master.[41] What vain imaginings the human heart can devise! Who could ever turn his face from the Mystery of God? For thirty years Bahá'u'lláh had trained the Bahá'ís to be steadfast in the Cause and in the Covenant. Now that He had taken His flight to the realm above, we were given the Kitáb-i-'Ahd, His Will and Testament, which placed 'Abdu'l-Bahá on the seat of His Covenant with all possible power and glory.

Strengthened by the Master, I traveled through to 'Ishqábád and Caucasia in order to raise the standard of the Covenant. I found the Bahá'ís in those places inflamed with the love of God. I warned them that no one, no matter how respected he may be, could claim a station equal to that of 'Abdu'l-Bahá. All agreed and were united, and signed a document confessing their faith.

FROM RUSSIA, I traveled to Beirut on my way to the Holy Land. Here I again met Jináb-i-Muḥammad Muṣṭafá Baghdádí. He was a mountain of strength and steadfastness. During my stay in Beirut this great soul (I owe my life to him) informed me of the secret plots against the Master in 'Akká. He revived my spirits and prepared me to attain the presence of the Center of the Covenant.

In 'Akká I did not go to visit anyone. My first action was to send a letter to 'Abdu'l-Bahá saying, "I know no one except the Master and have no desire to meet anyone unless He permits. I will not even enter the Shrines or circumambulate them without His permission." By the grace of God, on that very day I was able to make a pilgrimage to the Shrine of Bahá'u'lláh in the company of 'Abdu'l-Bahá and experienced the joy of hearing His melodious voice chanting the Tablet of Visitation.

THE READER should know that Muḥammad-'Alí, the half brother of 'Abdu'l-Bahá, even during the lifetime of his Father had transgressed against the station of servitude. Seeking to emerge from his relative obscurity and to claim some position for himself, he wrote letters and sent them secretly abroad. This caused the heart of Bahá'u'lláh infinite sorrow. The words of the Supreme Manifestation of God educated the whole of the Bahá'í world. He often remarked that Muḥammad-'Alí is a leaf on the Divine Lote Tree, which moves in accord with the breezes of God. Should it move away from this gentle breeze, it would wither and die.

Muḥammad-'Alí never wholeheartedly repented his action in writing these letters, but Bahá'u'lláh protected him and concealed his error. While he lived under the protection of Bahá'u'lláh, he remained relatively quiet, but the germ of dissension grew within him, and within some of his close associates.

When Jamál arrived in the Holy Land, after the ascension of Bahá'u'lláh, he met Muḥammad-'Alí. He also met Javád-i-Qazvíní, and they united in rebellion. They both assured Muḥammad-'Alí that all the Persian believers were obedient to Jamál and would be ready to turn to him at whatever moment he might choose. In this way, Muḥammad-'Alí could become the head of the Faith.

Such promptings fed the ego of Muḥammad-'Alí, and gradually he rose against his illustrious Brother. Those who were steadfast in the Covenant began to hear strange words. Whenever the plotters met with any of the Bahá'ís and found an opportunity to speak, they would warn: "Be careful. Do not believe in two Gods." This became like a frightening catchword. "Who believes in two Gods?" the friends asked one another. "Who has made this claim?"

The beloved Master showed increased love for the wavering souls and made life easier for them. But Muḥammad-'Alí and his companions did not pay any attention to the Master. They grudged no effort to humiliate Him and to create doubts in the hearts of those who were living in the Holy Land. Such champions of the Covenant as Muḥammad-Riḍá and Maḥmúd-i-Káshí repeatedly went to 'Abdu'l-Bahá's enemies and pointed out the explicit words revealed in the Will and Testament of Bahá'u'lláh. They openly and courageously warned Muḥammad-'Alí and his henchmen of the consequences of such nefarious deeds. They made it clear that disobedience is the fire of self-destruction, the smoke of which would inflame their own eyes.

'Abdu'l-Bahá suffered silently and never ceased His love and respectful treatment towards His enemies. At the banquets they all occupied the seats of honor around the table, while 'Abdu'l-Bahá stood and served. On many occasions we heard the Master give clear exhortations encouraging all to become united in the service of the Cause. He pleaded with them. But His words fell on deaf ears.

In those days, the friends' spiritual life, understanding, and growth depended upon the Tablets they received from the beloved Master, the visits of the pilgrims who gave them news of the Holy Land, and the letters from those who had the honor of living near the Shrines and serving the Center of the Covenant.

After the ascension of Bahá'u'lláh, a violent storm attacked the Faith of God and the believers everywhere. It created such a scorching fire and such suffocating smoke that many of the branches, boughs, and leaves which had grown on the Divine Lote Tree [42] were burned and consumed. They had eyes that could not see, ears that were unable to hear, and hearts that could no longer respond. It is a most lamentable situation when man becomes the captive of his own self. During His lifetime, Bahá'u'lláh taught the Bahá'ís to turn to Him when they did not understand any part of the Holy Writings. In His Will and Testament, He explicitly declared that in the absence of the Sun of Truth, the friends must turn to the Most Great Branch.[43] There were, however, a few who insisted on following their own egos and would not turn to 'Abdu'l-Bahá as the Center of Bahá'u'lláh's Covenant.

Fire, once it is ignited, stretches out its fiery tongue and will consume whoever dares to approach it or stand in its way. The sons of Bahá'u'lláh were caught in this merciless conflagration, as were some believers who had been outstanding pillars of the Cause in the days of Bahá'u'lláh, and others who would not shun them. Finally the Master remained almost alone. But even in His solitude He stretched forth His loving hands to rescue whoever was endangered by that fire. Letters, messengers, and loving exhortations constantly flowed from His presence.

However, as 'Abdu'l-Bahá increased His love and consideration for His enemies, He remained watchful and vigilant lest their words and letters reach the far-off friends whose hopes and aspirations were centered on the Holy Land and were sustained by letters from the believers living near the Holy Precincts. He did not wish that the friends throughout the world should learn of the shameful rebellion against the Covenant which was led by no less a person than His own half brother, Muḥammad-'Alí. Therefore, He forbade the friends to open any envelope which did not bear His own well-known seal.

The believers were vigilant and alert. For example, there was a physician in the city of Qazvín who was given the name "Hakím Illáhí" (Divine Physician) by 'Abdu'l-Bahá. He received a letter which carried the seal of the Master and he opened it. When he read the contents, he doubted their authenticity. The writer of the letter gave special instructions on how to address correspondence and suggested some satanic plans intended to overthrow the authority of the Master. The physician sent this letter back to the Holy Land and asked the Master, "Who is this person to instruct the friends? We all turn our hearts and souls to one point, and that is the beloved Master."

This letter from Hakím Illáhí uncovered the fact that the writer, Javád-i-Qazvíní, had first written an acceptable letter and placed it in an envelope. After the Master had affixed His seal to it, Javád had opened the envelope and inserted a different letter containing his own suggestions and evil thoughts.

The ever-moving pen of 'Abdu'l-Bahá saved the situation everywhere. The friends in the smallest villages and towns, in far-off districts in various countries, regularly received His inspiring messages. In their joy, they would copy them and send them wherever they could. Thus a continuous exchange of divine gifts was carried on all over the East. The friends busied themselves reading and transcribing the Tablets, encouraging one another, and warning the communities against the merciless attacks of the Covenant-breakers.

Thus the believers were protected against the infiltration of Covenant-breakers, with their misinterpretations of the Writings and their selfish ambitions. Should the Cause of God be entrusted to the hands of the people, we would find many interpreters in every town and village, and the light of true guidance would be extinguished. It would be as if a proficient physician wrote a catalog in which he listed the many kinds of illnesses and the herbs and medicines used to cure them. Would it then be enough to give this book to anyone who can read and ask him to attend a patient suffering from a serious disease? Would it be wise to follow the advice of anyone who could read this book? This is not enough. We need someone who can diagnose the illness and tell us what kind of medicine should be given—and how much, and at what times. Hence the Covenant of Bahá'u'lláh provides for the continuing guidance so necessary for the body of mankind.

There were many violators who vigorously attacked the Covenant and who traveled throughout the length and breadth of different countries. Yet they reaped no fruit but failure. Their odious arguments and evil attempts to undermine the Cause created some waves here and there, but ultimately the sea became calm, reflecting the shining Sun of Truth.

In Shíráz I met Salmán, the Messenger of the Merciful. To visit this great soul is a joy beyond measure for any of the believers. Though he was illiterate and his manner of life was extremely simple, he was the essence of intelligence and knowledge. Whenever the friends became entangled in some difficult question, he was able to answer the question and explain the matter under discussion in a few simple words. We never witnessed in him the slightest trace of self, which creeps so insidiously into the hearts of men. Salmán flattered no one, nor could he abide any compromise in matters pertaining to the Cause of God. The believers who were of pure character loved him and sought his presence. But there were a few who did not like him.

During one of his many visits to the Holy Land, the Ancient Beauty spoke to Salmán and said, "Respect the great ones in the meetings and do not belittle them."

To this he immediately replied, "No one except the Ancient Beauty and the Master is great to me. They may be big, but they are not great." His reward for this courageous reply was the sweet smile of Bahá'u'lláh.

Throughout the East, men and women of exceptional capacity and love arose to protect the friends of God against disunity and disobedience. Jináb-i-Afnán of Yazd stood like a mountain and never allowed the poisonous waters of the river of doubt to reach the tender shrubs which Bahá'u'lláh was cultivating. In Ardistán and the surrounding areas, the Rafí'á, Fatḥ-i-A'zam, and Majd families stood against the onslaught. In Iṣfahán, Jináb-i-Vazír was the champion of the Covenant of God.

The turbulent months passed, and the sun shone again on calmed and assured hearts. A new life began to stir. The Bahá'ís everywhere demonstrated signs of revival and joy after this destructive attack. Reports of unprecedented contributions and increased teaching activity were heard from all sides. Under the sunshine of the Covenant, the friends began to grow into maturity.

In Iṣfahán, Shaykh Najafí's thirst for the blood of the Bahá'ís had not diminished. He issued a death warrant for Jináb-i-Majd, one of the outstanding Bahá'ís of Ardistán. Madj was a tall, strong man. He was extremely firm in his faith, and he had a daring spirit which could strike fear into the hearts of the enemies of the Faith. When he heard that Najafí had signed and sealed his death warrant, he left Ardistán for Iṣfahán and walked up and down the most crowded streets and squares of that town. When the shaykh learned of this courageous behavior—how Majd had audaciously walked among the crowds in the most dangerous quarters of Iṣfahán—fear overtook him. He stopped going to the theological school, refused invitations, and even refrained from appearing in the mosque to lead the congregational prayers.

Some weeks passed, and Najafí continued to hear that his daring victim was still in Iṣfahán. Then he sent the believer a message: "Go home and do not breathe a word of this event to anyone." When Najafí was sure that Majd had returned to Ardistán, he renewed his public appearances.

It was about this time that I first witnessed the effect of the unifying power of the Word of God. During my teaching tour I reached Káshán, where the friends came from many different backgrounds: Jewish, Christian, Zoroastrian, and Muslim. But one could not tell them apart. Their unity was like water and perfume of rose: once mixed, it is impossible to distinguish one from the other.

In the city of Qum, I again met the Naddaf brothers and their newly converted friends. Strangely enough, these Muslim believers had been taught through the efforts of some Bahá'ís of Zoroastrian background who did business in Qum. It was a great privilege to visit Jináb-i-Ibn-i-Asdaq, who had just returned from the Holy Land. He arose like a giant to confirm the believers in the Covenant and arranged meetings every night to deepen the friends in the Cause of God.

However, in that region Jamál was like a thorn in the flesh of the believers. He would have liked nothing better than to become the leader of the Bahá'í community. Not only that—he did everything possible to extract money from the friends to support his son and relatives, who were like leeches attached to the Cause. The Hands of the Cause, the teachers, and all the Bahá'ís did their utmost to keep Jamál satisfied, but to no avail. The more they gave, the more he desired.

Dr. Muḥammad Khán, the son of Munajjim, was alert to the dangerous activities of Jamál. He warned the friends against him, saying, "I have known this man ever since my childhood. Since my father was well known as a Bahá'í at that time, he seldom appeared on the streets. But he regularly sent me to visit Jamál, inquire after his well-being, and bring him gifts. My father was always sad and worried about Jamál and often said that Jamál did not believe in anything. His sole aim is to gather fame and wealth. My father tried to keep him pacified, but he believed that it would have been much better if Jamál had never heard of the Faith.

"My father said that the friends should try to keep Jamál appeased. Should the smallest thing happen contrary to his plans and wishes, he could cause a great deal of trouble. My father was sure that if Jamál felt the least bit slighted he would go immediately to the 'ulamá in Ṭihrán, denounce the Faith, and assist in shedding the blood of innocent Bahá'ís."

Jinab-i-Afnán invited many of the friends to a meeting and requested that Jamál be present. The purpose of this meeting was to create unity and to inspire the friends to arise and serve the Cause. Jamál pretended to be steadfast in the Covenant and said, "Let us all write a letter to the Master and ask that He not call Himself 'Abdu'l-Bahá (the Servant of Bahá). Let Him continue to be called Sirru'lláh (the Mystery of God) as He was in the days of Bahá'u'lláh."

The friends were very much displeased with this presumptuous suggestion. One of them said, "He is the Center of the Covenant and He knows what to do. Who are we to tell Him what name or title He should adopt? We have accepted Bahá'u'lláh as the Supreme Manifestation of God. We know the Center of His Covenant under any name He chooses to be called."

A GROUP OF BELIEVERS AT THE TIME OF BAHÁ'U'LLÁH

Standing, from left to right: Ḥájí Mírzá Ḥaydar-'Alí, Jamál Effendi, Mírzá Abu'l-Qásim-i-Iṣfahání, Mis_h_qín Qalam, Muḥammad-Riḍáy-i-_Sh_írází Qannád, Mírzá Ja'far. Seated from left to right: Mírzá Maḥmúd-i-Kás_h_ání, Mírzá 'Abdu'l-Ra'úf, Mírzá Muḥsin Afnán, Mírzá Hádí Afnán (the father of Shoghi Effendi), Zaynu'l-Muqarrabín.

ḤÁJÍ MÍRZÁ ḤAYDAR-‘ALÍ
(second row, fourth from left)
with a group of Bahá’ís in the Holy Land at the time of ‘Abdu’l-Bahá

IN THE HOLY LAND I found the Center of Bahá'u'lláh's Covenant bereft of the companionship of the faithful. He was surrounded by those who desired nothing but to follow their own selfish desires and vain imaginings. I was astounded by the loving patience 'Abdu'l-Bahá showed toward these people. He never failed to provide them with whatever they demanded. Everyone knew that they made outrageous demands only for the purpose of forcing the Master into poverty and debt. Yet He accepted all such unkind treatment and met their demands, hoping only that they would not openly rise against the Faith and so cause unrest and distress in the infant Bahá'í communities around the world. Such a violent storm might prove fatal to the tender shoots growing in the vineyards of God. The Master respected all of the members of His family, protected them, and sought to guide them on the true path of faith.

For example, when my visit to 'Akká came to an end, 'Abdu'l-Bahá instructed me to travel to Iran by way of India. But before I left, He asked me to go to the Mansion of Bahjí to bid farewell to Muḥammad-'Alí and the family. He said, "You will be their guest during the whole night. About midnight Muḥammad-'Alí will ask you to be with him alone, as he desires to talk to you in private. When you answer his questions, be sure that you first ask permission from him. You must talk to him with love, courtesy, and respect. Utter nothing but that with which you will be inspired by God."

I went to Bahjí. It was late at night when Muḥammad-'Alí summoned me to his room. He asked his son to leave us alone and then stated, "I have a very private question to ask you. Don't you think that whatever my brother has inherited from Bahá'u'lláh, I have inherited, too?"

"Would you kindly grant me permission to answer?"

"Yes," he replied.

"In the Kitáb-i-Aqdas and in His Will and Testament, Bahá'u'lláh emphatically commanded the Branches, the Afnán, and all without exception to be obedient and submissive to the Most Great Branch. The more you obey, the higher will be your rank and position in the hearts of the believers. The station of the Branches and the Afnán is conditioned on their obedience to the Center of the Covenant. Since the Master was clearly given this great station, He must have something you do not have. Moreover, who is there in the world who can claim that he is comparable to the Master in any respect?"

At this point Muḥammad-'Alí got up and said, "It is time to sleep." Then he dismissed me. I slept in one of the lower rooms of the Mansion of Bahjí and returned to 'Akká the next day. I left Haifa for Bombay. But this experience showed me the crafty way in which the Covenant-breakers sowed the first seeds of doubt in the hearts of the believers.

IN ṬIHRÁN, Jináb-i-Adíb was a new Bahá'í. He had become a believer late in his life, but he was very mature, learned, audacious, and staunch in his faith. He was appointed a Hand of the Cause by Bahá'u'lláh. After the ascension of Bahá'u'lláh, but before the Kitáb-i-'Ahd (the Book of the Covenant) had reached Iran, Adíb had approached Jamál and asked him about the future leadership of the Faith. The arrogant Jamál replied that he knew that the Branches would share the leadership of the Faith.

Jináb-i-Adíb immediately protested that in the Kitáb-i-Aqdas, and in some other Tablets, Bahá'u'lláh had specifically mentioned that, after His passing, the believers must turn to only one person as the head of the Faith.

Jamál insisted, "There must be two Branches who will lead the believers and be the heads of the Faith."

"Then one must be silent and submissive; and one will speak and be the leader of the community," Adíb replied.

"No, both will speak," was Jamál's answer.

"This is against all standards of logic and reason," Adíb replied. "Even in worldly causes there cannot be two leaders at the head of any movement who share power between themselves. How much more must this be true of the Cause of God, which is based on a mighty foundation."

Since he could see that Adíb would not be convinced by his arguments, Jamál began to deny his position and to say that this was only something that he had heard from others. And the more Adíb protested, the more Jamál denied and relied on the excuse of his faulty hearing.

Jináb-i-Adíb was a mountain of steadfastness and sacrifice. Once he wrote a letter to the Grand Vazír of Iran explaining the Bahá'í position and giving clear and obvious proofs that Bahá'ís shun all political activities and are obedient to their governments. He signed his name and his title to this letter and openly stated that it was his religious duty to report these things to the state.

I considered the fact that I had enjoyed fifty years of happiness in the shadow of the Faith, while Adíb was a new believer who had already sacrificed so much. So, since the danger was obvious, I proposed that this letter should be copied by Maḥmúd-i-Zarqaní and sent in my name, because we needed Adíb and we did not want to run the risk of losing him, or having him become entangled in the many difficulties which could result from such a letter. My suggestion was agreed to, and the letter was sent through the mail. In due time we received an acknowledgment signed by the secretary of the Grand Vazír. The entire letter was eventually cabled to the crown prince who was then on his way to Ṭihrán.

This was one of the greatest services which Jináb-i-Adíb rendered to the Cause of God. His letter protected the Bahá'ís from suspicion and from the slanderous reports which, like torrents of hate, might cover the whole country during times of convulsion and upheaval. Bahá'u'lláh later praised the justice of the Grand Vazír who received this letter and acted so fairly.

The Hand of the Cause Mullá 'Alí-Akbar was well known as a Bahá'í by the people. For years, whenever he passed through the streets or the public squares, he would be abused with curses and foul words. A certain Mullá Riḍá was a neighbor of this Hand of the Cause and he started a campaign against the Faith. He maliciously attacked the Bahá'ís and encouraged the people to kill Bahá'ís and plunder their property. He singled out Mullá 'Alí-Akbar for special attack.

In order to protect this friend, the other Hands met in the house of Jináb-i-Ibn-i-Asdaq. They consulted on what to do and concluded that during the first part of the month of Muḥarram, when religious sentiment among Muslims would be high, Mullá 'Alí-Akbar should change his residence and make no public appearances until the period of commotion and chaos was over.

They then invited the Hand to attend this meeting, and one of those present explained the results of the consultation. Mullá 'Alí-Akbar showed himself to be the epitome of faith, devotion, and steadfastness. He smiled and said, "In His many Tablets, 'Abdu'l-Bahá has advised us to observe wisdom. But this means submission, and not fear and hiding. It means solidarity in plans of action, truthfulness and forbearance, and that the seeds of faith should be sown in fertile soil.

"I have been arrested more than ten times, put in chains, and placed in prison. Often there did not appear to be any hope of my release. On one occasion I was in prison for three years. People who were less well known than I were honored with the cup of martyrdom, while I am still alive. If martyrdom is to be my destiny, what greater end! If it is the decree and the will of God, why hide and be afraid?" All of us were greatly heartened by this explanation, every word of which gave us more understanding and assurance.

THE TIME CAME when I had to leave Ṭihrán for other parts. I traveled to Qazvín and to Tabríz, and then to 'Ishqábád.

In Qazvín, though this city was the center of Jamál's evil plots, I found the friends steadfast and faithful and firm in the Covenant. In Tabríz, with the exception of two persons, all others were steadfast in the Covenant. Bahá'í meetings were held every day. In some places the friends had donated gardens, houses, and land to the Faith. Letters received from the Holy Land which were not signed or sealed by the Master would immediately be sent back to 'Akká. It seemed that Muḥammad-

'Alí was doing his utmost to penetrate this citadel of the Covenant. But in all cases he met impenetrable barriers and found no way to disturb the beloved friends, who remained safe and secure in the shade of the Tree of Life, under the shadow of the Most Great Branch.

While in Caucasia I learned that Jamál had finally revealed his true self. The friends had begun to realize his burning ambition. It became known that he had written a letter to 'Abdu'l-Bahá and had demanded three things: that he be appointed as the head of the Faith in Persia, that 'Abdu'l-Bahá prepare a special house for him and his son, and that the Master rebuke the Hands of the Cause for their behavior toward him. This letter remained unanswered.

Jamál became furious that the Bahá'ís of Persia did not turn to him and instead remained steadfast in the Covenant of Bahá'u'lláh. He wrote letters to the outstanding Bahá'ís of the country complaining and bewailing the fact that they would not assist him with his plans. Such deeds of pride and profanity made the Bahá'ís realize that Jamál never had a particle of faith. The friends from then on shunned him and would not even walk on the street where he lived.

There is an important lesson in the story of Jamál. In the eyes of the friends he had been a very important person. When he entered the homes of the friends, the bed he slept on and even the chairs he used would be regarded as special objects. The friends used to kiss his hand. He would say to the people, "The kissing of hands is forbidden. But for the glory of the Cause, I will not prevent the believers from prostrating themselves in front of me and kissing my hand." However, when these same people learned that the object of their adoration had become a Covenant-breaker, they did not even allow him to enter their homes.

When Jamál had failed in all his plans, I wrote him

a short letter and said, "An ignorant person may claim that there is no God. But God keeps the whole universe functioning in perfect order, without allowing anyone to break this order. Now reflect on the many schemes you have devised to reach your goal. Reflect also on the fact that all of these plans have been thwarted. None have produced the desired result. Is this not sufficient evidence that your aims and desires are opposed to the order of God, the Fashioner of the universe?" The friends gave him my note, but I received no reply.

AFTER PASSING THROUGH Caucasia I went to Beirut. From there I made my way to the Holy Land. The beloved Master's first instruction to me was this: "Do not mention Jamál and his misdeeds."

I said, "But he has written pamphlets to refute the Covenant of God and they are being spread everywhere."

"Yes," 'Abdu'l-Bahá replied, "but he has not signed them. As long as he does not openly proclaim himself as the author of these works, we will not denounce his name and his wrongdoing. We must always conceal the faults of others."

Some days after my arrival, 'Abdu'l-Bahá instructed the pilgrims to go to Bahjí. The Master came by Himself, on foot, and slowly approached the Shrine of Bahá'u'lláh. After tea, He instructed all of us to stand in a circle around the Shrine and wait for Him to come out. He said that even if we heard curses and foul words, or if we were pelted with stones, we must not pay any attention.

This actually happened. The Covenant-breakers who lived in the Mansion next to the Shrine, those people without God or religion, cursed us and stoned us. Even so, that day was so wondrous that it is an everlasting memory which, whenever I recall it, enkindles my heart and soul.

It was heartbreaking for us to learn about the evil work of the Covenant-breakers and their malicious attacks on the beloved Master. These things were never related to any of the friends abroad. But being in the Holy Land, I could see what burdens of sorrow they laid on the Master's shoulders every day.

These enemies were able to approach the mayor of 'Akká and bribe him. They asked that he exile 'Abdu'l-Bahá from the city of 'Akká, thinking that after His departure the pilgrims would come to them and would consider them as the center of the Cause. However, the mayor of 'Akká was soon dismissed and sent back to his own country.

At another time they offered one of Bahá'u'lláh's cloaks and a pair of his spectacles to the governor of Haifa. They encouraged him to go and visit 'Abdu'l-Bahá with the cloak on his shoulders and with the glasses. When he came, 'Abdu'l-Bahá realized that he was wearing things which had belonged to His Father, and He was deeply grieved. However, He did not say a word and treated the man with His usual extreme courtesy and love. That day passed, but the time came when that same governor was put in prison and in chains. It was 'Abdu'l-Bahá who hastened to help and liberate him. After receiving such unexpected kindness, he begged for forgiveness saying, "It was not my fault. Your enemies misled me into taking such a grievious step."

DURING THE FIRST WEEK of my pilgrimage, early one morning, Mírzá Áqá Ján, who had been the amanuensis of Bahá'u'lláh, came in and made funny gestures. He said, "Alláh-u-Abhá! You have an illumined gathering."

I left the room, but he followed me to another room and said the same thing. I went to another room, and he again followed and said the same thing. I returned to the first room and he came with me. Again he said, "Alláh-u-Abhá! You have an illumined gathering."

Another believer and I left the house and made our way to a shop in the street. Áqá Ján followed us, hopping up and down and saying the Greatest Name. We went to one of the shops which was owned by a believer, and he followed us and stood outside repeating the same thing. A crowd gathered before we had left the shop. But still Áqá Ján followed us, hopping and saying the Greatest Name. This continued until after midday.

When the mayor of 'Akká learned that Áqá Ján had disturbed us and others, he sent soldiers to arrest him. He was taken to the governor's house. The mayor sent the following message to the Master: "We are sending soldiers to Yemen. The boat is anchored in the port and is ready to sail. If you approve, I will banish this person to Yemen."

'Abdu'l-Bahá's response was immediate. "This would not please me," he replied.

Mírzá Áqá Ján was released, but he never ceased to cause fresh troubles for the Master. At one time he even sent news to the Covenant-breakers and to the friends that Bahá'u'lláh had appeared to him in a dream and had promised to help him if he arose at the appointed hour to conquer the Bahá'í world and displace the Most Great Branch. Even the Covenant-breakers once decided to kill him and destroy his body with fire, but 'Abdu'l-Bahá always protected him.

It often happened that when the Master went to the Shrine of His Father, either riding or on foot, the governor and his officials would follow Him to the surrounding area of Bahjí. These people would have tea and refreshments while the Master, followed by the friends, would pay homage at the resting place of Bahá'u'lláh. Many times they observed the Master carrying loads of earth in His cloak for the gardens around the Shrine. At other times they observed Him carrying a water pot on His shoulders.

Twice a year for about six years, 'Abdu'l-Bahá would take at least one hundred flower pots from the Riḍván Garden to Bahjí. It was the most exciting procession. 'Abdu'l-Bahá would carry a flower pot on His shoulder, and all the friends and pilgrims would follow Him two by two with flower pots on their shoulders. Mírzá Maḥmúd-i-Káshí would walk in front of the friends and chant prayers in a loud and melodious voice. Once the commander of the army, accompanied by his officers, passed by and saw this spiritual procession. He said to the Master, "This is the Army of the Kingdom, and these are the angels of the Exalted Realm."

I remember one evening, as the commemoration of the Ascension of Bahá'u'lláh approached, the Master prepared two hundred lanterns. One of these contained twenty candles, and each of the others two candles. It was about sunset when the same procession of friends, carrying these lanterns, made their way to Bahjí. It happened that we passed a camp of soldiers. The officers stood in their places and paid their respect to the Master. We were all in tears. When we reached the Shrine, there were two rows of worshipers: the friends in one row, and the officers with their soldiers in the other. Everyone was in tears. When the pilgrimage came to an end, the officers encircled the Master. They were served tea and refreshments. This was one of the most memorable nights of my life. Every particle in the air and on the earth seemed both to absorb and reflect the glory and majesty of the Kingdom of God.

The Covenant-breakers could not bear to see such glorious acts of servitude. They hastened to the Muslim clergy in 'Akká and expressed their objection to such demonstrations of homage to the resting place of Bahá'u'lláh.

On that evening, 'Abdu'l-Bahá remained awake all night. The friends could not separate themselves from Him and gathered in the Pilgrim House adjacent to the Shrine. Sometimes tea or coffee was served. But the most lamentable part of it was when dawn approached. We all went to the Shrine for a second time. To our horror we discovered that Mírzá Áqá Ján was there and had taken up residence in the Shrine. It was evident that 'Abdu'l-Bahá's heart was burning with anguish, but He remained silent. He approached the Shrine but chose to sit in the sandy place that surrounded it. About two hundred friends sat in a circle with Him as we remembered the days we had all spent in the presence of the Ancient Beauty.

All of a sudden, Mírzá Áqá Ján dashed out of the Shrine, barefooted and bareheaded, and dressed in a shroud of mourning. He threw dust on his head and gesticulated wildly. He kept repeating, "My Beloved! My Beloved! Where are you?" His behavior was so silly that we could not control our laughter. The Covenant-breakers who had occupied the Mansion next door tried repeatedly to take him away, but he kept returning. Again and again he dashed into our circle, repeating some of the verses of Bahá'u'lláh. He seemed like a drunken man who could not keep his balance. He kept shouting, running, and reciting parts of the Tablets in an irreverent manner. A short while later we all dispersed. Yet despite all this, 'Abdu'l-Bahá continued to respect Áqá Ján, and protect him, and care for him.

ONE OF 'ABDU'L-BAHÁ'S major services to the Cause of God was to transfer the remains of the Báb from Persia to the Holy Land, and to place them in the Shrine on the side of Mount Carmel. This act was the fulfilment of the prophecies recorded in the Holy Books about the glory of Carmel and the surrounding areas.

The Báb's wooden casket had been placed in the house of Jináb-i-Vazír in Iṣfahán. It was well hidden in the house, and no one knew its location. When the time came, the beloved Master issued orders that the body should be transferred from Persia to the Holy Land.

Those responsible were advised to travel first to Iraq. They arrived in Baghdád with their sacred cargo, entrusted it to the hands of the friends there, and, after visiting the Shí'ih shrines, returned home. My cousin, Ḥusayn-i-Vakíl, acted as a custodian of the casket in Baghdád. Further instructions were received that the Báb's remains were to be sent to Beirut and others were given the honor of this task. Finally, the box containing the Divine Trust was placed in the hands of the Master.

Let us look back for a moment to the early days when the Master took the first steps to purchase the land on Mount Carmel where Bahá'u'lláh had indicated the Tomb of the Báb should stand. When the Covenant-breakers learned that He intended to purchase that land, their malicious opposition was aroused. They approached the owner of the land and persuaded him not to sell. They assured him that in a short time the land would be worth ten times its value. They instigated others to write letters to the government claiming possession of all the land on Mount Carmel. Therefore, it took the Master more than six months of persistent effort to purchase the desired piece of land. But even so, that land was situated like an island in the midst of other land which belonged to other people. There was no access to it. The Master was so weighed down with troubles that He decided not to pursue the matter. During His silence, the Covenant-breakers became more active than ever. But the Master left everything in the hands of God. Time passed, and the Covenant-breakers were happy because they thought that they had been completely successful.

One day a person who owned land adjacent to the land for the Shrine of his own free will sought the presence of 'Abdu'l-Bahá. When he met with the Master, he told Him of all the intrigues of the enemies of the Cause. He expressed his deep regrets, begged the forgiveness of 'Abdu'l-Bahá, and declared his readiness to sell whatever land was desired.

The Master immediately began making plans for the construction of the Báb's Tomb. When the enemies learned of these efforts, they wrote letters to the Ottoman court reporting that 'Abdu'l-Bahá was planning to build a huge fortress on the side of Mount Carmel. They asserted that this fort would be a great danger to the safety of the empire. The government immediately ordered all work on the construction of the Shrine to cease. Such orders were given, not once, but several times. The Master appealed the case to a government committee of investigation, which eventually gave permission for the construction to continue.

Some of the friends lost their patience and suggested to the Master, "Why don't you explain the whole situation to the government?"

"Impossible!" the Master answered. "How can I explain these things to anyone? I would have to complain against the members of my own family. Then what would people say? They would surely say that a great Prophet had come for the purpose of bringing all people to unity, but the members of His own family are now fighting among themselves.

"This fatal disease must be fought with patience and forgiveness. Whatever wrongdoing I mention in my Tablets is only to help the friends to become more steadfast, and to strengthen those who are weak, that they might become firm and courageous believers. God is the greatest of all helpers; we surrender our affairs into His hands. We must be occupied with our own work and tread the path of servitude, detached from all else but God. Whoever walks this path will surely reap the fruits of his patience and forbearance, and will be counted as my companion in the service of His Threshold. Those who deviate from this path will surely find regret.

"We must supplicate our Lord so that He, in His unlimited bounty, may forgive our sins, accept our prayers of repentance, and awaken all men to the light of true understanding."

'Abdu'l-Bahá undertook to prepare a suitable depository for the priceless remains of the Báb. He instructed the friends of Rangoon, Burma, to make a hardwood coffin and a marble sarcophagus. The marble was to be unique and of brilliant luster. When these were prepared, the Master instructed that the top and sides of the sarcophagus were to be adorned with the Greatest Name. The designs were prepared in exquisite penmanship by the calligrapher, Mishkín-Qalam.

When the friends in Burma were ready to ship their work to 'Akká, they brought two carts and walked the whole distance to the seashore, pulling the carts and chanting along the way. Their procession was joined by many others. Then they placed their precious trusts in a mosque, and crowds of people were attracted by the jubilation. They inquired about the reason for such joyous ceremonies. One of the friends took the floor and told them of the life of the Báb, His martyrdom, and His burial on Mount Carmel. Many hearts were touched, and many entered the Faith and joined the friends in serving the Cause in Burma.

THERE WAS not a moment's rest for the Master. At times He seemed like a man on a ship in the middle of a tempestuous ocean. But this would never cause 'Abdu'l-Bahá to lose heart. He never appeared despondent or hopeless. That was not the Master. Out of the darkness He would emerge time and again with a new plan and a new victory.

Not even having finished the Shrine, He called on the friends to raise the first Bahá'í House of Worship in the heart of Asia, in 'Ishqábád, Russia. A cousin of the Báb, Jináb-i-Afnán,[44] was appointed by 'Abdu'l-Bahá to go to 'Ishqábád from his native town of Yazd to oversee the construction of the Temple. Upon his arrival the consul general of Iran, the governor of the province, merchants, and other notables joined the Bahá'ís in receiving their honored guest. The governor expressed joy and gratitude that the first Bahá'í House of Worship would be erected under his dominion.

Preparations for construction were soon under way. Once the plans had been approved, the friends immediately set to work to build the Temple. The cornerstone was laid in place by a representative of the Czar himself. Most of the Temple was completed within four years.

AT THIS TIME 'Abdu'l-Bahá instructed me to take a trip to Caucasia and to 'Ishqábád. I had the honor of visiting Jináb-i-Afnán and being in his presence. He was the embodiment of perfection and sanctity. He had both spiritual gifts and administrative skill. He spent all his gifts to carry out the mission conferred upon him by the Master. He sacrificed most of his fortune to erect the House of Worship. I could see clearly that Jináb-i-Afnán was hardly in this world and did not belong to it. He would pay only scant attention to his personal and worldly affairs. Yet he remained rich, and his wealth would always meet all his needs.

The time came when I decided to bid farewell to the friends in 'Ishqábád and travel to Mashhad. There I met Maḥmúd-i-Zarqání. We shared a house together and worked together for the Faith. We associated with all classes of people, and before long our teaching activities became so well known that people came to us with all kinds of problems which had nothing to do with the Faith. Whoever came in, by the grace of God returned home happy and contented.

Our teaching was so successful that some people

feared that within one year all the important people of the city would become Bahá'ís. Bahá'í teachers from other areas came to help with this effort. Meetings were held all over the city, and the believers formed committees to feed the poor and advance the public welfare.

We were still in Khurásán when we heard of the great upheaval in Yazd. This news caused uneasiness among the new believers of Mashhad. The disturbances lasted for more than two months during which 195 believers were mercilessly put to death. The governor of the province, instead of protecting the people under his care, ruthlessly helped the bloodthirsty mobs. Bahá'ís were killed, their houses destroyed, and their possessions plundered or confiscated.

During these disorders, a well-known maidservant of the Cause, 'Alavíyyih Khánum, reached the city of Yazd. As soon as she set foot in the town she was arrested and made to undergo all kinds of persecutions. Eventually the chief of police took her under his protection and gave her some advice: "Won't you just speak one word of denial and rid yourself of all this suffering?"

"Under no circumstances," she replied. "That one word would deprive me of all the eternal bounties of God. I will gladly sacrifice this ephemeral life for the supremacy of the Name of God." The governor heard about her imprisonment and issued an order that she should be sent to Ábádih.

During all these disturbances no one in the whole of Iran, or in the neighboring countries, would listen to the cries of the Bahá'ís for justice. The beloved friends were at the mercy of the irresponsible mobs who were encouraged by the bloodthirsty clergy and the most ignorant of governors. The only One who stretched forth His hand to assist the wronged and sorrow-stricken victims was the Master, Who was Himself a prisoner, incarcerated in the city of 'Akká and surrounded by the most despicable enemies. He looked after the urgent needs of the children and youth, the old men and women who were caught in the fire of persecution.

THE COVENANT-BREAKERS continually conspired against 'Abdu'l-Bahá. They formed groups against Him and, like vipers, began to move in different directions. The groups approached the governor, the secret police, the outstanding 'ulamá, and any other person they could influence in Palestine, Syria, or Turkey. They did everything they could to arouse the officials against 'Abdu'l-Bahá.

The Master remained calm and serene. He never approached the authorities. He suffered in silence. He prayed fervently for His enemies, that they might open their eyes and cease committing iniquities against the innocent band of believers in 'Akká.

Whenever 'Abdu'l-Bahá received any gift, He would immediately send it to His family who had violated the Covenant of God. Far from being grateful, they in turn would offer these gifts to the governor, the commander of the army, or others, in an effort to convince them to take steps against 'Abdu'l-Bahá. Their aim was to have the Master exiled to a distant and unknown place. If this could be accomplished, they believed that, since they would be in possession of the Holy Shrines, all of the believers would regard them as the center of the Faith.

The most active of the Covenant-breakers was Majd-i-Dín, the cousin of the Master. He was the center of abominable deeds. He would sneer at the pilgrims who visited 'Abdu'l-Bahá and declare, "You are only here for a few days. Soon you will leave and everything will fall into our hands. All will seek shelter under our shadow."

'Abdu'l-Bahá liked to visit the resting place of His Father every week. But in order to appease the emnity of Muḥammad-'Alí and his supporters, He decided to remain in 'Akká. When He desired to visit Bahjí, He would go up to the roof of His house, face the Shrine of Bahá'u'lláh, and pray. He would sometimes chant the Tablet of Visitation in a loud voice. We would hear Him chanting, and we were indeed heartbroken. This situation continued for two years.

The result of all the complaints and mischief of the Covenant-breakers was an upheaval of debris which buried everyone. An order came from the officials that all members of the family were to live in 'Akká, and no one was to step outside the city. The Master was already residing in 'Akká, so it was the Covenant-breakers living in Bahjí who were now forced to return to 'Akká and to live there. They were all taken to the city and placed under restriction. The officials soon realized that it was Muḥammad-'Alí and Majd-i-Dín who had caused all the trouble. But 'Abdu'l-Bahá intervened on their behalf and requested the authorities to allow them to return to Bahjí.

ONE GOVERNOR came to power who was the essence of courtesy and faith. He loved 'Abdu'l-Bahá to the point of worship. In addition Badrí Big, the military commander, was very friendly to the Master. When the enemies of the Cause saw this state of affairs, they became furious and joined all their forces to bring about the downfall of 'Abdu'l-Bahá.

They decided to send false reports, containing the most alarming accusations, to the Ottoman court. They claimed that the governor as well as the military commander and his officers had all become the servants of 'Abdu'l-Bahá. They were accused of training thirty thousand soldiers, of raising a flag of rebellion inscribed with the Greatest Name, and of convincing the Arab tribes of the desert to join this rebellion. The Covenant-breakers claimed that 'Abdu'l-Bahá had proclaimed Himself to be the Return of Christ and, as such, claimed sovereignty over all the nations of the world and regarded all rulers as His vassals.

'Abdu'l-Bahá sent a single sentence in reply to these accusations: "Listen to the reports, but ask the accusers to present their evidence and their witnesses." But the court accepted the reports without investigation. The reason for this was that the accusing letters had been signed and sealed by the brothers and cousins of 'Abdu'l-Bahá.

Before long, the thick clouds of confusion and persecution again covered the horizon of 'Akká. The friends and supporters of the Master were unexpectedly dismissed from their posts. When the noble governor came to the Master to bid Him farewell, 'Abdu'l-Bahá assured him that the governor would return to high position in the future and that the bounties of God would rain down upon him. The military commander was also shorn of his rank, but he remained happy and content that he had served the Master.

New officials were placed in charge of the telegraph and post offices. All letters were opened and read, and every telegram was scrutinized. Secret police were everywhere. People were ordered to stay at home in the evening. The enemies of the Faith were jubliant.

The Master remained alone. He even asked the friends to leave 'Akká and to disperse in different directions. Danger threatened Him from all sides, yet He retained His tranquillity and fortitude. He began to repair the house in which He lived and to plant grape vines in His small garden.

Letters of accusation regularly found their way to the court of the sultan in Constantinople. Although such reports should have been investigated, not even one of the believers was consulted. All of the reports were taken to be true, and a committee of four men was dispatched to 'Akká to confirm the charges.

No sooner had these high officials set foot on the shore at 'Akká than the Covenant-breakers clustered around them. They entertained the committee members in the most flattering way and offered them costly presents. Gifts were constantly sent to them. Though the enemies received no promises, their hearts were full of hope. They expected that 'Abdu'l-Bahá would soon be exiled.

'Abdu'l-Bahá never approached the members of the committee. This enraged the officials. In order to show their contempt for the Master, they sent a summons for " 'Abbás" to appear before them. Upon receiving this order, 'Abdu'l-Bahá went to the place where the committee held its meetings. The room was crowded with the enemies of the Faith.

The Master said, "I am happy and proud that you referred to me as simply ' 'Abbás.' This is the way that the Prophets of God are addressed. Who has heard of Moses Pá<u>sh</u>á, or Jesus Big, or Muḥammad <u>Kh</u>án? They are called simply Moses, Jesus, and Muḥammad."

The officials were astounded by this audacious statement. One of them inquired, "We have heard that you have books in your house which are dangerous to the public welfare."

'Abdu'l-Bahá answered, "No such books are ever found in my possession."

The same officer declared, "But there are witnesses who have testified to this fact."

'Abdu'l-Bahá rose from his seat. He said, "I told you that I do not have such writings in my house, and that is all." Then He left the room. The committee was amazed at the courage of this man whom they believed to be completely at their mercy.

The joy and excitement of the Covenant-breakers was unbounded. And the sorrow of the believers overflowed. A few of the friends and the faithful members of 'Abdu'l-Bahá's family urged Him to flee 'Akká by ship, and the captain of one boat expressed his readiness to carry Him to whatever port He wished. But the Master responded that the Báb did not run away and abandon the arena of sacrifice. Bahá'u'lláh did not run away. Neither would He try to flee from danger.

As the members of the committee of investigation boarded their ship to return to Constantinople, they were happy and satisfied. They were impatient to reach the sultan's court and relate the results of their investigation. They saw this as an opportunity to present themselves as the protectors of the throne and the defenders of the empire. One of them announced to his collaborators, "My reward for this investigation will be the governorship of Damascus. The very first act I will perform after taking office will be to hang 'Abdu'l-Bahá from the gate of 'Akká."

But before the committee could reach its destination and present its libelous report, the foundations of the Ottoman Empire began to crumble and the realm was thrown into confusion. The committee and all its reports were totally ignored. All the evil efforts of these corrupt officials were brought to naught.

We are amazed when we realize that thousands of persons were put to death all over the empire because of the mere accusation by a spy or secret agent that they were disloyal. What grave danger was caused for the Master by the accusations of His own family, the false reports and rumors circulated about Him, and the investigation of a hostile committee from the sultan's own court! It is the most astounding fact that 'Abdu'l-Bahá should have remained alive after these repeated attacks from all sides. Can we not see the hand of God operating in the whole universe?

NOW, at the end of my life, all I possess is ignorance and weakness and unawareness and heedlessness and neglect and valuelessness and worthlessness and uselessness and poverty and shamelessness and destitution and powerlessness and disobedience and wrongdoing and sin and darkness and worldliness and transience and selfishness and corrupt desire. Any wrongdoing or sin which can be imagined is mine.

I do not write this from a sense of humility. This is only truth and honesty and reality. The bounties of God are obvious and apparent. Fifty years ago in Adrianople I attained the presence of that Sun of Truth before Whom all others must prostrate themselves. From that time, every breath I have taken I have tried to conform to His will, and every step I have taken I have directed toward Him. I do not know if my services were acceptable to Him, but His compassion and love and generosity have always surrounded me. My worst deeds were met with the greatest compassion. The more I transgressed, the more He concealed my faults. The more I sought after my own vain imaginings, the more He showed me the light of His Spirit. The more I erred, the more generous He was. He saved me from the greatest difficulties, and from the calamity of self.

All humanity must follow some occupation, from kings and sultans to servants and slaves. Everyone is surrounded by misery and trouble. A just king will have more trouble than any of his subjects; a fair chief will face more difficulties than any of his underlings. Just to earn a living and to gain their daily bread, some people have chosen years of exile. Moreover, for the sake of greed, many of the rich and the learned have placed their lives in danger continually. And all this only to follow their own ambitions in quest of the mirage of prestige and honor. How often have others, on account of their own crimes and corruption, been placed in prison and suffered exile or been captured, enslaved, or executed! And I am only one of these people. Whatever evil caused such ones to commit crimes for which they were punished was also part of me. How grateful I am that I was protected, and my sins were concealed, and I was not put to shame. If I burn every second, I can never repay His forgiveness and mercy. I am utterly impotent.

All that I have comes from the Cause of God. The believers respected me as a teacher, but I did not deserve such respect. They were all the true teachers of the Faith. They would face the problems of the world to earn a living, and then spend their earnings on those like me who could travel and teach. Then we were called the promulgators of the Faith. But we made no sacrifices; we only received. In the Name of God, those noble believers sacrificed everything for us. I, and others like me, reached the highest degree of honor and happiness without struggle or sacrifice. I can only pray that the mercy and generosity of God, which has followed me over thousands of miles, will also accompany me in the future.

Now it has been ten years, more or less, that by the grace and bounty of the Master I have lived under the shadow of mercy in the Holy Land, and have partaken every day of the manna from heaven, and have seen what Moses saw on Sinai. I thank God that I have attained and have witnessed the kindness and the generosity and the servitude of the believers—virtues which are but a drop when compared to the kindness and compassion of 'Abdu'l-Bahá and the Greatest Holy Leaf[45] and the Holy Mother.[46]

A true Bahá'í I am not. O God! Assist me and make my efforts fruitful. Assist the Master! This book I have written by His order. But I am so old and decrepit that many times while writing I have forgotten the order of my words and lost my train of thought. When this happened, I would have to get up and leave my work. But whenever I started to write again, my pen would carry on the story. This humble servant has never entered any school and is unaware of the rules of grammar and style.

I beseech all the Bahá'ís (may my soul be sacrificed for them) to beg for my forgiveness at the Holy Threshold, as I see nothing in myself but wrongdoing, and nothing among the servants of God but forgiveness and concealment.

With thanks to God, the Lord of the worlds.

May 17, 1912

EPILOGUE

The author of these memoirs, Ḥájí Mírzá Ḥaydar-'Alí, who is known as the "Angel of Carmel" by the Bahá'ís of the West, was indeed close to the heart of 'Abdu'l-Bahá. During His journeys to America, the Master sent some of His most tender messages to this veteran soldier of the Cause. In one of them He describes the meetings which were held, the banquets, the newly recruited believers, and after each comment He repeats, "I miss you very much."

What finally happened to Ḥaydar-'Alí? There were many requests from all over the Bahá'í world for him to visit. But as he advanced in years the Master did not approve his going abroad. He would often wrap Ḥaydar-'Alí in His cloak and lovingly repeat, "Ḥájí is ours! Ḥájí is ours!"

He was asked by the Master to teach the children of His household. All the grandsons of 'Abdu'l-Bahá attended these classes. Shoghi Effendi, who was later to become the Guardian of the Faith, was among his students. Ḥaydar-'Alí recognized his station even at this early age. Whenever the young Shoghi Effendi would enter the class, Ḥájí Mírzá Ḥaydar-'Alí would rise in respect for his student. He often whispered in his ear, "Sufficient to you is the school of the Master."

In many of the group photographs which were taken of the pilgrims in Haifa during the time of 'Abdu'l-Bahá, two old men can be seen standing on opposite sides of the group. One of these is Ḥájí Mírzá Ḥaydar-'Alí and the other is Mullá Abú-Ṭálib, a veteran believer from Caucasia.

Ḥaydar-'Alí and Abú-Ṭálib would often exchange jokes with one another in Haifa, to the delight of all of the friends. These two veteran soldiers in the twilight of their lives were still so lively that they could make everyone laugh.

When Ḥaydar-'Alí became ill and bedridden, the beloved Master would go to his room and inquire about his health and well-being. One day He asked him, "How do you sleep at night?"

"Not very well," the Ḥájí replied.

Mullá Abú-Ṭálib immediately interrupted and said, "He is wrong. He snores all night long!" And the Master and the friends laughed most heartily.

'Abdu'l-Bahá commanded that two of the believers should help Ḥájí Mírzá Ḥaydar-'Alí walk in the sunshine every morning. Once his cousin, Vakíl, took him by the arm to help him walk. He asked the Ḥájí, "What else do you desire? The beloved Master comes to see you every day and grants you the strength to carry the burden of life."

Ḥaydar-'Alí smiled and said, "If you really love me, pray that I will die steadfast in the Covenant and . . ."

Before he finished his sentence, his cousin interrupted and exclaimed, "What do you mean, dear cousin! You are almost ninety years old, and so much loved and respected by the Master!"

"Yes, that is true," was the reply. "But you cannot imagine how very cunning and insidious the self can be. It accompanies a man to the edge of the grave. The only thing that protects us from its deadly grasp is the divine assistance which is granted through prayer."

The next day, when the Master visited the Ḥájí, He assured Ḥaydar-'Alí, saying, "You will sleep well. You will sleep well."

NOTES

1. Ḥájí Muḥammad Karím Khán was a student of Siyyid Káẓim. He assumed a position of leadership among the Shaykhís in Iran after the siyyid's death, and became a bitter enemy of the Báb.
2. A title of the Shí'ih Muslim clergy.
3. Mullá Zaynu'l-'Abidín, surnamed Zaynu'l-Muqarrabín (Ornament of Them that Are Nigh unto God) by Bahá'u'lláh was a Shí'ih mujtahid before becoming a Bábí. He later became an outstanding follower of Bahá'u'lláh.
4. Jináb is a polite title meaning honorable. The name of the person referred to follows immediately after this title.
5. Shaykh Aḥmad and Siyyid Káẓim were the two leaders of the Shaykhí School who anticipated the imminent appearance of the Báb.
6. Ṣubḥ-i-Azal, Mírzá Yaḥyá, the half brother of Bahá'u'lláh who eventually rebelled against Him and became the "Arch-Breaker of the Covenant of the Báb" (see *God Passes By*, p. 233). Azal was nominated by the Báb as His successor, "as a figurehead pending the manifestation of the Promised One" (*God Passes By*, p. 28).
7. Shí'ih Muslims believe that the Imám Mihdí, the Twelfth Imám, did not die, but went into hiding for a thousand years. He lives in a secret place and will reappear at the time of the end to establish justice and righteousness on earth. The Báb fulfilled these prophecies with His declaration in 1844.
8. A classic epic of mystic poems, consisting of six volumes, composed in the thirteenth century by Jalálu'd-Dín Rúmí.
9. The surname Afnán (Twig) designates relatives of the Báb.
10. See *Memorials of the Faithful*, pp. 108–16.
11. See *Memorials of the Faithful*, pp. 5–8.
12. Now a city in Iraq, Karbilá is the place where the Imám Ḥusayn, the rightful successor of the Prophet Mu-

ḥammad, fought a hopeless battle against his enemies and was martyred, along with many of his followers, in 680 A.D.

13. The Shrine of Shaykh Ṭabarsí is the place where a few hundred Bábís withstood the siege of the Persian army from October 1848 to May 1849. The Bábís were finally lured from their makeshift fort when the enemy swore an oath of peace on the Qur'án, and were massacred.
14. Bahá'u'lláh.
15. Siyyid Muḥammad, the Antichrist of the Bahá'í Revelation, joined with Ṣubḥ-i-Azal in rebellion against Bahá'u'lláh.
16. See *Epistle to the Son of the Wolf,* p. 73, and *God Passes By,* p. 178.
17. The son of Jacob. See Qur'án, Sura 12, and Genesis, chapters 37–50. The Qur'án states: "And when they saw him they were amazed at him, and cut their hands, and said, 'God keep us! This is no man! This is no other than a noble angel!' " (Sura 12:31, Rodwell translation).
18. The verse of the Qur'án reads (Sura 112):

    Say: He is God alone:
    God the eternal!
    He begetteth not, and He is not begotten;
    And there is none like unto Him.
    (Rodwell translation)

19. A reference to Jalálu'd-Dín Rúmí, who founded the order of dancing dervishes in the thirteenth century.
20. The house of retreat and worship for a dervish order.
21. The faithful brother of Bahá'u'lláh.
22. The ruler of Egypt who acted as the viceroy of the sultan of Turkey.
23. Two Bábís attempted unsuccessfully to assassinate Náṣiri'd-Dín Sháh in 1852. See *God Passes By,* pp. 62–63.
24. The name of Bahá'u'lláh (Bahá). The two most widely used forms of the Greatest Name are Yá Bahá'u'l-Abhá, an invocation, and Alláh-u-Abhá, a greeting. Both of these are referred to as the Greatest Name.
25. The phrase "people of the path" is used here in the Islamic sense to denote people of true religion.
26. See Foreword, p. vi.

27. This place should not be confused with the other garden (also known as the Garden of Riḍván) in Iraq where Bahá'u'lláh first revealed His Mission.
28. See note 21.
29. 'Abdu'l-Bahá.
30. That is, 'Abdu'l-Bahá.
31. *The Hidden Words of Bahá'u'lláh,* Arabic No. 42, p. 13.
32. When the Imám Ḥusayn and his band of warriors were besieged on the plains of Karbilá, their enemies denied them access to water, even though they were dying of thirst and the Euphrates River was within their sight. The Shí'ihs remember this as a heinous crime. (See note 12.)
33. A cube-like, stone building in Mecca. At the time of Muḥammad it was a pagan shrine. Muḥammad destroyed all the idols housed in it after His conquest of Mecca, and made it a place of pilgrimage for all Muslims.
34. Mírzá 'Alí-Muḥammad, surnamed Varqá (Dove) by Bahá'-u'lláh. He was an outstanding Bahá'í poet and teacher. He and his twelve-year-old son, Rúhu'lláh, were both eventually martyred.
35. See note 9.
36. The honorific titles of two Bábí brothers who were prominent citizens of Iṣfahán. They were denounced by the Muslim clergy of the city and were martyred.
37. The illustrious Bahá'í scholar. He was sent to the United States by 'Abdu'l-Bahá and is well known as the author of *The Bahá'í Proofs.*
38. One of the titles of 'Abdu'l-Bahá.
39. See *'Abdu'l-Bahá: The Center of the Covenant of Bahá'u'lláh* by H. M. Balyuzi, p. 526, note 58. Reference is made there to an Englishman who embraced the Faith in Persia, and who was an official of the Indo-European Telegraph Company. This may be the same individual mentioned here by Ḥájí Mírzá Ḥaydar-'Alí.
40. The term Branches (Aghṣán) refers to the male descendants of Bahá'u'lláh. One of the titles of 'Abdu'l-Bahá is "The Most Great Branch." Here, "Branches" refers to Bahá'u'lláh's sons.
41. That is, Mírzá Muḥammad-'Alí, the Arch-Breaker of Bahá'u'lláh's Covenant.
42. "Divine Lote Tree" is a symbolic reference to the Manifestation of God, Bahá'u'lláh.

43. ‘Abdu’l-Bahá.
44. Ḥájí Mírzá Muḥammad-Taqí-i-Afnán. See *Memorials of the Faithful*, pp. 126–29.
45. Bahíyyih Khánum, the sister of ‘Abdu’l-Bahá.
46. Munírih Khánum, the wife of ‘Abdu’l-Bahá.